THE WILL TO CHANGE

Also by bell hooks

Ain't I a Woman: Black Women and Feminism
Feminist Theory: From Margin to Center
Talking Back: Thinking Feminist, Thinking Black
Yearning: Race, Gender, and Cultural Politics
Breaking Bread: Insurgent Black Intellectual Life
Black Looks: Race and Representation
Sisters of the Yam: Black Women and Self-Recovery
Teaching to Transgress: Education as the Practice of Freedom
Outlaw Culture: Resisting Representations
Art on My Mind: Visual Politics
Killing Rage: Ending Racism
Reel to Real: Race, Sex, and Class at the Movies
Bone Black: Memories of Girlhood, Vol. 1
Wounds of Passion: A Writing Life
Remembered Rapture: The Writer at Work
Happy to Be Nappy
All about Love: New Visions
Feminist Theory: From Margin to Center
Where We Stand: Class Matters
Salvation: Black People and Love
Communion: The Female Search for Love
Rock My Soul: Black People and Self-Esteem

THE WILL TO CHANGE

MEN, MASCULINITY, AND LOVE

bell hooks

WASHINGTON SQUARE PRESS
New York London Toronto Sydney

Washington Square Press
1230 Avenue of the Americas
New York, NY 10020

ISBN 978-0-7434-5608-1

First Washington Square Press trade paperback edition January 2005

50

WASHINGTON SQUARE PRESS and colophon are trademarks of Simon & Schuster, Inc.

Manufactured in the United States of America

For information regarding special discounts for bulk purchases, please contact Simon & Schuster Special Sales at 1-800-456-6798 or business@simonandschuster.com.

"Alchemically transforming lead into true gold, men are given the opportunity to burn, to be touched by an inner fire, to live a life of substance, to be changed utterly."

This book is dedicated to the memory of my grandfather, Gus Oldham—burning, a heart on fire, whose love, stronger than death, illuminates.

In our rapidly changing society we can count on only two things that will never change. What will never change is the will to change and the fear of change. It is the will to change that motivates us to seek help. It is the fear of change that motivates us to resist the very help we seek.

—Harriet Lerner, *The Dance of Intimacy*

Contents

PREFACE

About Men

When Phyllis Chesler's book *About Men* was first published more than ten years ago, I was excited. At last, I thought then, a feminist thinker will explain this mystery—men. Back then I had never shared with anyone the feelings I had about men. I had not been able to confess that not only did I not understand men, I feared them. Chesler, with her usual "take no prisoners" daring, I was certain, would not simply name this fear, explain it, she would do much more: she would make men real to me. Men would become people I could talk to, work with, love. Her book was disappointing. Filled with quotes from numerous sources, newspaper clippings of male violence, it offered bits and pieces of information; there was little or no explanation, no interpretation. From that time on I began to think that women were afraid to speak openly about men, afraid to explore deeply our connections to them—what we have witnessed as daughters, sisters, grandmothers, mothers, aunts, lovers, occasional sex objects—and afraid even to acknowledge our ignorance, how much we really do not know about men. All that we do not know intensifies our sense of fear and threat. And certainly to know men only in relation to male violence, to the violence inflicted upon women and children, is a partial, inadequate knowing.

Nowadays I am amazed that women who advocate feminist politics have had so little to say about men and masculinity. Within the early writings of radical feminism, anger, rage, and even hatred of men was voiced, yet there was no meaningful attempt to offer ways to resolve these feelings, to imagine a culture of reconciliation where women and men might meet and find common ground. Militant feminism gave women permission to unleash their rage and hatred at men but it did not allow us to talk about what it meant to love men in patriarchal culture, to know how we could express that love without fear of exploitation and oppression.

Before her death Barbara Deming was among those rare outspoken feminist thinkers who wanted to create a space for women to talk openly about our feelings about men. Articulating her concern that the wellspring of female fury at men was making it impossible for women to express any other feelings than their sense that "men are hopeless," she stated: "It scares me that more and more women are coming to feel this way, to feel that men as an entire gender are hopeless." Deming did not feel that men were incapable of change, of moving away from male domination, but she did feel that it was necessary for women to speak the truth about how we think about men: "I believe that the only way we can get where we have to go is by never refusing to face the truth of our feelings as they rise up in us—even when we wish it were not the truth. So we have to admit to the truth that we sometimes wish our own fathers, sons, brothers, lovers were not there. But, this truth exists alongside another truth: the truth that this wish causes us anguish." While some women active in the feminist movement felt anguished about our collective inability to convert masses of men to feminist thinking, many women simply felt that feminism gave them permission to be indifferent to men, to turn away from male needs.

When contemporary feminism was at its most intense, many women insisted that they were weary of giving energy to men, that they wanted to place women at the center of all feminist discussions. Feminist thinkers, like myself, who wanted to include men in the discussion were usually labeled male-identified and dismissed. We were "sleeping with the enemy." We were the feminists who could not be trusted because we cared about the fate of men. We were the feminists who did not believe in female superiority any more than we believed in male superiority. As the feminist movement progressed, the fact became evident that sexism and sexist exploitation and oppression would not change unless men were also deeply engaged in feminist resistance, yet most women were still expressing no genuine interest in highlighting discussions of maleness.

Acknowledging that there needed to be more feminist focus on men did not lead to the production of a body of writing by women about men. The lack of such writing intensifies my sense that women cannot fully talk about men because we have been so well socialized in patriarchal culture to be silent on the subject of men. But more than silenced, we have been socialized to be the keepers of grave and serious secrets—especially those that could reveal the everyday strategies of male domination, how male power is enacted and maintained in our private lives. Indeed, even the radical feminist labeling of all men as oppressors and all women as victims was a way to deflect attention away from the reality of men and our ignorance about them. To simply label them as oppressors and dismiss them meant we never had to give voice to the gaps in our understanding or to talk about maleness in complex ways. We did not have to talk about the ways our fear of men distorted our perspectives and blocked our understanding. Hating men was just another way to not take men and masculinity seriously. It was simply easier for feminist women to talk about challenging and changing patriarchy than it was for us to talk about men—what we knew and did not know, about the ways we wanted men to change. Better to just express our desire to have men disappear, to see them dead and gone.

Eloquently, Barbara Deming expresses this longing when she writes about her father's death: "Years ago now. It was on a weekend in the country and he'd been working outside with a pick and a shovel, making a new garden plot. He'd had a heart attack and fallen there in the loose dirt. We'd called a rescue squad, and they were trying to bring him back to life, but couldn't. I was half-lying on the ground next to him, with my arms around his body. I realized that this was the first time in my life that I had felt able to really touch my father's body. I was holding hard to it—with my love—and with my grief. And my grief was partly that my father, whom I loved, was dying. But it was also that I knew already that his death would allow me to feel freer. I was mourning that this had to be so. It's a grief that is hard for me to speak of. That the only time I would feel free to touch him without feeling threatened by his power over me was when he lay dead—it's unbearable to me. And I think there can hardly be a woman who hasn't felt a comparable grief. So it's an oversimplification to speak the truth that we sometimes wish men dead—unless we also speak the truth which is perhaps even harder to face (as we try to find out own powers, to be our own women): the truth that this wish is unbearable to us. It rends us." As a young woman in my twenties who had not yet found her own powers, I often wished the men in my life would die. My longing for my father's death began in childhood. It was the way I responded to his rage, his violence. I used to dream him gone, dead and gone.

Death was the way out of the fear evoked by the proclamation "Wait until your father comes home." The threat of punishment was so intense, his power over us so real. Lying in my girlhood bed waiting to hear the hard anger in his voice, the invasive sound of his commands, I used to think, "If only he would die, we could live." Later as a grown woman waiting for the man in my life to come home, the man who was more often than not a caring partner but who sometimes erupted into violent fits of rage, I used to think, "Maybe he will have an accident and die, maybe he will not come home, and I will be free and able to live." Women and children all over the world want men to die so that they can live. This is the most painful truth of male domination, that men wield patriarchal power in daily life in ways that are awesomely life-threatening, that women and children cower in fear and various states of powerlessness, believing that the only way out of their suffering, their only hope is for men to die, for the patriarchal father not to come home. Women and female and male children, dominated by men, have wanted them dead because they believe that these men are not willing to change. They believe that men who are not dominators will not protect them. They believe that men are hopeless.

When I left home and went away to college, if I called home and my father answered, I hung up. I had nothing to say to him. I had no words to communicate to the dad who did not listen, who did not seem to care, who did not speak words of tenderness or love. I had no need for the patriarchal dad. And feminism had taught me that I could forget about him, turn away from him. In turning away from my dad, I turned away from a part of myself. It is a fiction of false feminism that we women can find our power in a world without men, in a world where we deny our connections to men. We claim our power fully only when we can speak the truth that we need men in our lives, that men are in our lives whether we want them to be or not, that we need men to challenge patriarchy, that we need men to change.

While feminist thinking enabled me to reach beyond the boundaries set by patriarchy, it was the search for wholeness, for self-recovery, that led me back to my dad. My reconciliation with my father began with my recognition that I wanted and needed his love—and that if I could not have his love, then at least I needed to heal the wound in my heart his violence had created. I needed to talk with him, to tell him my truth, to hold him close and let him know he mattered. Nowadays when I call home, I revel in the sound of my father's voice, his southern speech familiar and broken in all the right places. I want to hear his voice forever. I do not want him to die, this dad whom I can hold in my arms, who receives my love and loves me back. Understanding him, I understand myself better. To claim my power as a woman, I have to claim him. We belong together.

The Will to Change: Men, Masculinity, and Love is about our need to live in a world where women and men can belong together. Looking at the reasons patriarchy has maintained its power over men and their lives, I urge us to reclaim feminism for men, showing why feminist thinking and practice are the only way we can truly address the crisis of masculinity today. In these chapters I repeat many points so that each chapter alone will convey the most significant ideas of the whole. Men cannot change if there are no blueprints for change. Men cannot love if they are not taught the art of loving.

It is not true that men are unwilling to change. It is true that many men are afraid to change. It is true that masses of men have not even begun to look at the ways that patriarchy keeps them from knowing themselves, from being in touch with their feelings, from loving. To know love, men must be able to let go the will to dominate. They must be able to choose life over death. They must be willing to change.

THE WILL
TO CHANGE

1

Wanted: Men Who Love

Every female wants to be loved by a male. Every woman wants to love and be loved by the males in her life. Whether gay or straight, bisexual or celibate, she wants to feel the love of father, grandfather, uncle, brother, or male friend. If she is heterosexual she wants the love of a male partner. We live in a culture where emotionally starved, deprived females are desperately seeking male love. Our collective hunger is so intense it rends us. And yet we dare not speak it for fear we will be mocked, pitied, shamed. To speak our hunger for male love would demand that we name the intensity of our lack and our loss. The male bashing that was so intense when contemporary feminism first surfaced more than thirty years ago was in part the rageful cover-up of the shame women felt not because men refused to share their power but because we could not seduce, cajole, or entice men to share their emotions—to love us.

By claiming that they wanted the power men had, man-hating feminists (who were by no means the majority) covertly proclaimed that they too wanted to be rewarded for being out of touch with their feelings, for being unable to love. Men in patriarchal culture responded to feminist demand for greater equity in the work world and in the sexual world by making room, by sharing the spheres of power. The place where most men refused to change—believed themselves unable to change—was in their emotional lives. Not even for the love and respect of liberated women were men willing to come to the table of love as equal partners ready to share the feast.

No one hungers for male love more than the little girl or boy who rightfully needs and seeks love from Dad. He may be absent, dead, present in body yet emotionally not there, but the girl or boy hungers to be acknowledged, recognized, respected, cared for. All around our nation a billboard carries this message: "Each night millions of kids go to sleep starving—for attention from their dads." Because patriarchal culture has already taught girls and boys that Dad's love is more valuable than mother love, it is unlikely that maternal affection will heal the lack of fatherly love. No wonder then that these girls and boys grow up angry with men, angry that they have been denied the love they need to feel whole, worthy, accepted. Heterosexual girls and homosexual boys can and do become the women and men who make romantic bonds the place where they quest to find and know male love. But that quest is rarely satisfied. Usually rage, grief, and unrelenting disappointment lead women and men to close off the part of themselves that was hoping to be touched and healed by male love. They learn then to settle for whatever positive attention men are able to give. They learn to overvalue it. They learn to pretend that it is love. They learn how not to speak the truth about men and love. They learn to live the lie.

As a child I hungered for the love of my dad. I wanted him to notice me, to give me his attention and his affections. When I could not get him to notice me by being good and dutiful, I was willing to risk punishment to be bad enough to catch his gaze, to hold it, and to bear the weight of his heavy hand. I longed for those hands to hold, shelter, and protect me, to touch me with tenderness and care, but I accepted that this would never be. I knew at age five that those hands would acknowledge me only when they were bringing me pain, that if I could accept that pain and hold it close, I could be Daddy's girl. I could make him proud. I am not alone. So many of us have felt that we could win male love by showing we were willing to bear the pain, that we were willing to live our lives affirming that the maleness deemed truly manly because it withholds, withdraws, refuses is the maleness we desire. We learn to love men more because they will not love us. If they dared to love us, in patriarchal culture they would cease to be real "men."

In her moving memoir *In the Country of Men* Jan Waldron describes a similar longing. She confesses that "the kind of father I ached for I have never seen except in glimpses I have embellished with wishful imaginings." Contrasting the loving fathers we long for with the fathers we have, she expresses the hunger:

> Dad. It is a vow against all odds, in the face of countless examples to the contrary. Dad. It does not have the utilitarian effect of Mum or Ma. It's still spoken as a ballad refrain. It's a pledge that originates in the heart and fights for life amid the carnage of persistent, obvious history to the contrary and excruciatingly scant follow-through. Mother love is aplenty and apparent: we com-

> plain because we have too much of it. The love of a father is an uncommon gem, to be hunted, burnished, and hoarded. The value goes up because of its scarcity.

In our culture we say very little about the longing for father love.

Rather than bringing us great wisdom about the nature of men and love, reformist feminist focus on male power reinforced the notion that somehow males were powerful and had it all. Feminist writing did not tell us about the deep inner misery of men. It did not tell us the terrible terror that gnaws at the soul when one cannot love. Women who envied men their hardheartedness were not about to tell us the depth of male suffering. And so it has taken more than thirty years for the voices of visionary feminists to be heard telling the world the truth about men and love. Barbara Deming hinted at those truths:

> I think the reason that men are so very violent is that they know, deep in themselves, that they're acting out a lie, and so they're furious at being caught up in the lie. But they don't know how to break it.... They're in a rage because they are acting out a lie—which means that in some deep part of themselves they want to be delivered from it, are homesick for the truth.

The truth we do not tell is that men are longing for love. This is the longing feminist thinkers must dare to examine, explore, and talk about. Those rare visionary feminist seers, who are now no longer all female, are no longer afraid to openly address issues of men, masculinity, and love. Women have been joined by men with open minds and big hearts, men who love, men who know how hard it is for males to practice the art of loving in patriarchal culture.

In part, I began to write books about love because of the constant fighting between my ex-boyfriend Anthony and myself. We were (and at the time of this writing still are) each other's primary bond. We came together hoping to create love and found ourselves creating conflict. We decided to break up, but even that did not bring an end to the conflict. The issues we fought about most had to do with the practice of love. Like so many men who know that the women in their lives want to hear them declare love, Anthony made those declarations. When asked to link the "I love you" words with definition and practice, he found that he did not really have the words, that he was fundamentally uncomfortable being asked to talk about emotions.

Like many males, he had not been happy in most of the relationships he had chosen. The unhappiness of men in relationships, the grief men feel about the failure of love, often goes unnoticed in our society precisely because the patriarchal culture really does not care if men are unhappy. When females are in emotional pain, the sexist thinking that says that emotions should and can matter to women makes it possible for most of us to at least voice our heart, to speak it to someone, whether a close friend, a therapist, or the stranger sitting next to us on a plane or bus. Patriarchal mores teach a form of emotional stoicism to men that says they are more manly if they do not feel, but if by chance they should feel and the feelings hurt, the manly response is to stuff them down, to forget about them, to hope they go away. George Weinberg explains in *Why Men Won't Commit:* "Most men are on quest for the ready-made perfect woman because they basically feel that problems in a relationship can't be worked out. When the slightest thing goes wrong, it seems easier to bolt than talk." The masculine pretense is that real men feel no pain.

The reality is that men are hurting and that the whole culture responds to them by saying, "Please do not tell us what you feel." I have always been a fan of the *Sylvia* cartoon where two women sit, one looking into a crystal ball as the other woman says, "He never talks about his feelings." And the woman who can see the future says, "At two P.M. all over the world men will begin to talk about their feelings—and women all over the world will be sorry."

If we cannot heal what we cannot feel, by supporting patriarchal culture that socializes men to deny feelings, we doom them to live in states of emotional numbness. We construct a culture where male pain can have no voice, where male hurt cannot be named or healed. It is not just men who do not take their pain seriously. Most women do not want to deal with male pain if it interferes with the satisfaction of female desire. When feminist movement led to men's liberation, including male exploration of "feelings," some women mocked male emotional expression with the same disgust and contempt as sexist men. Despite all the expressed feminist longing for men of feeling, when men worked to get in touch with feelings, no one really wanted to reward them. In feminist circles men who wanted to change were often labeled narcissistic or needy. Individual men who expressed feelings were often seen as attention seekers, patriarchal manipulators trying to steal the stage with their drama.

When I was in my twenties, I would go to couples therapy, and my partner of more than ten years would explain how I asked him to talk about his feelings and when he did, I would freak out. He was right. It was hard for me to face that I did not want to hear about his feelings when they were painful or negative, that I did not want my image of the strong man truly challenged by learning of his weaknesses and vulnerabilities. Here I was, an enlightened feminist woman who did not want to hear my man speak his pain because it revealed his emotional vulnerability. It stands to reason, then, that the masses of women committed to the sexist principle that men who express their feelings are weak really do not want to hear men speak, especially if what they say is that they hurt, that they feel unloved. Many women cannot hear male pain about love because it sounds like an indictment of female failure. Since sexist norms have taught us that loving is our task whether in our role as mothers or lovers or friends, if men say they are not loved, then we are at fault; we are to blame.

There is only one emotion that patriarchy values when expressed by men; that emotion is anger. Real men get mad. And their mad-ness, no matter how violent or violating, is deemed natural—a positive expression of patriarchal masculinity. Anger is the best hiding place for anybody seeking to conceal pain or anguish of spirit. My father was an angry man. At times he still is, even though he is past eighty years old. Recently when I called home he said, speaking of me and my sister, "I love you both dearly." Amazed to hear Dad speak of love, I wanted us to talk but I could not find words. Fear silenced me, the old fear of Dad the patriarch, the silent, angry man and the new fear of breaking this fragile bond of caring connection. So I could not ask, "What do you mean, Dad, when you tell me that you love me dearly?" In the chapter focusing on our search for loving men in *Communion: The Female Search for Love* I make this observation: "Lots of women fear men. And fear can lay the foundation for contempt and hatred. It can be a cover-up for repressed, killing rage." Fear keeps us away from love. And yet women rarely talk to men about how much we fear them.

My siblings and I have never talked with Dad about the years he held us hostage—imprisoning us behind the walls of his patriarchal terrorism. And even in our adult years we are still afraid to ask him, "Why, Daddy? Why were you always so angry? Why didn't you love us?"

In those powerful passages where she writes of her father's death, Barbara Deming names that fear. As death is swiftly taking him beyond her reach, she sees clearly that fear had kept him away from her all along—his fear of her being too close, and her fear of seeking to be close to him. Fear keeps us from being close to the men in our lives; it keeps us from love.

Once upon a time I thought it was a female thing, this fear of men. Yet when I began to talk with men about love, time and time again I heard stories of male fear of other males. Indeed, men who feel, who love, often hide their emotional awareness from other men for fear of being attacked and shamed. This is the big secret we all keep together—the fear of patriarchal maleness that binds everyone in our culture. We cannot love what we fear. That is why so many religious traditions teach us that there is no fear in love.

We struggle then, in patriarchal culture, all of us, to love men. We may care about males deeply. We may cherish our connections with the men in our lives. And we may desperately feel that we cannot live without their presence, their company. We can feel all these passions in the face of maleness and yet stand removed, keeping the distance patriarchy has created, maintaining the boundaries we are told not to cross. In a class with students who are reading the trilogy of books I have written about love, with forty men talking about love, we talk of fathers. A black male in his late thirties, whose father was present in the home, a hard worker, talked about his recent experience of parenthood, his commitment to be a loving father, and his fear that he will fail. He fears failure because he has not had a loving role model. His father was almost always away from home, working, roaming. When he was home, his favorite way of relating was to tease and taunt his son mercilessly, in a biting voice full of sarcasm and contempt, a voice that could humiliate with just a word. Reflecting the experience of many of us, the individual telling his story talked about wanting the love of this hard man but then learning not to want it, learning to silence his heart, to make it not matter. I asked him and the other men present, "If you have closed off your heart, shut down your emotional awareness, then do you know how to love your sons? Where and when along the way did you learn the practice of love?"

He tells me and the other men who sit in our circle of

love, "I just think of what my father would do and do the opposite." Everyone laughs. I affirm this practice, adding only that it is not enough to stay in the space of reaction, that being simply reactive is always to risk allowing that shadowy past to overtake the present. How many sons fleeing the example of their fathers raise boys who emerge as clones of their grandfathers, boys who may never even have met their grandfathers but behave just like them? Beyond reaction, though, any male, no matter his past or present circumstance, no matter his age or experience, can learn how to love.

In the past four years the one clear truth I have learned from individual men I have met while traveling and lecturing is that men want to know love and they want to know how to love. There is simply not enough literature speaking directly, intimately, to this need. After writing a general book about love, then one specifically about black people and love, then another focusing on the female search for love, I wanted to go further and talk about men and love.

Women and men alike in our culture spend very little time encouraging males to learn to love. Even the women who are pissed off at men, women most of whom are not and maybe never will be feminist, use their anger to avoid being truly committed to helping to create a world where males of all ages can know love. And there remains a small strain of feminist thinkers who feel strongly that they have given all they want to give to men; they are concerned solely with improving the collective welfare of women. Yet life has shown me that any time a single male dares to transgress patriarchal boundaries in order to love, the lives of women, men, and children are fundamentally changed for the better.

Every day on our television screens and in our nation's newspapers we are brought news of continued male violence at home and all around the world. When we hear that teenage boys are arming themselves and killing their parents, their peers, or strangers, a sense of alarm permeates our culture. Folks want to have answers. They want to know, Why is this happening? Why so much killing by boy children now, and in this historical moment? Yet no one talks about the role patriarchal notions of manhood play in teaching boys that it is their nature to kill, then teaching them that they can do nothing to change this nature—nothing, that is, that will leave their masculinity intact. As our culture prepares males to embrace war, they must be all the more indoctrinated into patriarchal thinking that tells them that it is their nature to kill and to enjoy killing. Bombarded by news about male violence, we hear no news about men and love.

Only a revolution of values in our nation will end male violence, and that revolution will necessarily be based on a love ethic. To create loving men, we must love males. Loving maleness is different from praising and rewarding males for living up to sexist-defined notions of male identity. Caring about men because of what they do for us is not the same as loving males for simply being. When we love maleness, we extend our love whether males are performing or not. Performance is different from simply being. In patriarchal culture males are not allowed simply to be who they are and to glory in their unique identity. Their value is always determined by what they do. In an antipatriarchal culture males do not have to prove their value and worth. They know from birth that simply being gives them value, the right to be cherished and loved.

I write about men and love as a declaration of profound gratitude to the males in my life with whom I do the work of love. Much of my thinking about maleness began in childhood when I witnessed the differences in the ways my brother and I were treated. The standards used to judge his behavior were much harsher. No male successfully measures up to patriarchal standards without engaging in an ongoing practice of self-betrayal. In his boyhood my brother, like so many boys, just longed to express himself. He did not want to conform to a rigid script of appropriate maleness. As a consequence he was scorned and ridiculed by our patriarchal dad. In his younger years our brother was a loving presence in our household, capable of expressing emotions of wonder and delight. As patriarchal thinking and action claimed him in adolescence, he learned to mask his loving feelings. He entered that space of alienation and antisocial behavior deemed "natural" for adolescent boys. His six sisters witnessed the change in him and mourned the loss of our connection. The damage done to his self-esteem in boyhood has lingered throughout his life, for he continues to grapple with the issue of whether he will define himself or allow himself to be defined by patriarchal standards.

At the same time that my brother surrendered his emotional awareness and his capacity to make emotional connection in order to be accepted as "one of the boys," rejecting the company of his sisters for fear that enjoying us made him less male, my mother's father, Daddy Gus, found it easier to be disloyal to patriarchy in old age. He was the man in my childhood who practiced the art of loving. He was emotionally aware and emotionally present, and yet he also was trapped by a patriarchal bond. Our grandmother, his wife of more than sixty years, was always deeply invested in the dominator model of relationships. To macho men Daddy Gus, Mama's father, appeared to be less than masculine. He was seen as henpecked. I can remember our patriarchal father expressing contempt for Daddy Gus, calling him weak—and letting Mama know via domination that he would not be ruled by a woman. Dad took Mama's admiration for her dad, for his capacity to love, and made it appear that what was precious to her was really worthless.

Back then Mama did not know how lucky she was to have a loving father. Like so many females, she had been seduced by myths of romantic love to dream of a strong, domineering, take-control, dashing, and daring man as a suitable mate. She married her ideal only to find herself trapped in a bond with a punishing, cruel, unloving patriarchal man. She spent more than forty years of marriage believing in the patriarchal gender roles that told her he should be the one in control and that she should be the one to submit and obey. When patriarchal men are not cruel, the women in their lives can cling to the seductive myth that they are lucky to have a real man, a benevolent patriarch who provides and protects. When that real man is repeatedly cruel, when he responds to care and kindness with contempt and brutal disregard, the woman in his life begins to see him differently. She may begin to interrogate her own allegiance to patriarchal thinking. She may wake up and recognize that she is wedded to abuse, that she is not loved. That moment of awakening is the moment of heartbreak. Heartbroken women in longtime marriages or partnerships rarely leave their men. They learn to make an identity out of their suffering, their complaint, their bitterness.

Throughout our childhood Mama was the great defender of Dad. He was her knight in shining armor, her beloved. And even when she began to see him, to really see him, as he was and not as she had longed for him to be, she still taught us to admire him and be grateful for his presence, his material provision, his discipline. A fifties woman, she was willing to cling to the fantasy of the patriarchal ideal even as she confronted the brutal reality of patriarchal domination daily. As her children left home, leaving her alone with her husband, her hope that they might find their way to love was soon dashed. She was left face-to-face with the emotionally shut down cold patriarch she had married. After fifty years of marriage she would not be leaving him, but she would no longer believe in love. Only her bitterness found a voice; she now speaks the absence of love, a lifetime of heartache. She is not alone. All over the world women live with men in states of lovelessness. They live and they mourn.

My mother and father were the source figures who shaped my patterns of love and longing. I spent most of the years between twenty and forty seeking to know love with intellectually brilliant men who were simply emotionally unaware, men who could not give what they did not have, men who could not teach what they did not know—men who did not know how to love. In my forties I began a relationship with a much younger man who had been schooled in the art and practice of feminist thinking. He was able to acknowledge having a broken spirit. As a child he had been a victim of patriarchal tyranny. He knew there was something wrong within, even though he had not yet found a language to articulate what was missing.

"Something missing within" was a self-description I heard from many men as I went around our nation talking about love. Again and again a man would tell me about early childhood feelings of emotional exuberance, of unrepressed joy, of feeling connected to life and to other people, and then a rupture happened, a disconnect, and that feeling of being loved, of being embraced, was gone. Somehow the test of manhood, men told me, was the willingness to accept this loss, to not speak it even in private grief. Sadly, tragically, these men in great numbers were remembering a primal moment of heartbreak and heartache: the moment that they were compelled to give up their right to feel, to love, in order to take their place as patriarchal men.

Everyone who tries to create love with an emotionally unaware partner suffers. Self-help books galore tell us that we cannot change anyone but ourselves. Of course they never answer the question of what will motivate males in a patriarchal culture who have been taught that to love emasculates them to change, to choose love, when the choice means that they must stand against patriarchy, against the tyranny of the familiar. We cannot change men but we can encourage, implore, and affirm their will to change. We can respect the truth of their inner being, a truth that they may be unable to speak: that they long to connect, to love, to be loved.

The Will to Change: Men, Masculinity and Love answers the

questions about love asked by men of all ages in our culture. I write in response to questions about love asked me by the men I know most intimately who are still working to find their way back to the open-hearted, emotionally expressive selves they once were before they were told to silence their longings and close their hearts.

The Will to Change is the offering I bring to the feast of male reclamation and recovery of self, of their emotional right to love and be loved. Women have believed that we could save the men in our lives by giving them love, that this love would serve as the cure for all the wounds inflicted by toxic assaults on their emotional systems, by the emotional heart attacks they undergo every day. Women can share in this healing process. We can guide, instruct, observe, share information and skills, but we cannot do for boys and men what they must do for themselves. Our love helps, but it alone does not save boys or men. Ultimately boys and men save themselves when they learn the art of loving.

2

Understanding Patriarchy

Patriarchy is the single most life-threatening social disease assaulting the male body and spirit in our nation. Yet most men do not use the word "patriarchy" in everyday life. Most men never think about patriarchy—what it means, how it is created and sustained. Many men in our nation would not be able to spell the word or pronounce it correctly. The word "patriarchy" just is not a part of their normal everyday thought or speech. Men who have heard and know the word usually associate it with women's liberation, with feminism, and therefore dismiss it as irrelevant to their own experiences. I have been standing at podiums talking about patriarchy for more than thirty years. It is a word I use daily, and men who hear me use it often ask me what I mean by it.

Nothing discounts the old antifeminist projection of men as all-powerful more than their basic ignorance of a major facet of the political system that shapes and informs male identity and sense of self from birth until death. I often use the phrase "imperialist white-supremacist capitalist patriarchy" to describe the interlocking political systems that are the foundation of our nation's politics. Of these systems the one that we all learn the most about growing up is the system of patriarchy, even if we never know the word, because patriarchal gender roles are assigned to us as children and we are given continual guidance about the ways we can best fulfill these roles.

Patriarchy is a political-social system that insists that males are inherently dominating, superior to everything and everyone deemed weak, especially females, and endowed with the right to dominate and rule over the weak and to maintain that dominance through various forms of psychological terrorism and violence. When my older brother and I were born with a year separating us in age, patriarchy determined how we would each be regarded by our parents. Both our parents believed in patriarchy; they had been taught patriarchal thinking through religion.

At church they had learned that God created man to rule the world and everything in it and that it was the work of women to help men perform these tasks, to obey, and to always assume a subordinate role in relation to a powerful man. They were taught that God was male. These teachings were reinforced in every institution they encountered—schools, courthouses, clubs, sports arenas, as well as churches. Embracing patriarchal thinking, like everyone else around them, they taught it to their children because it seemed like a "natural" way to organize life.

As their daughter I was taught that it was my role to serve, to be weak, to be free from the burden of thinking, to caretake and nurture others. My brother was taught that it was his role to be served; to provide; to be strong; to think, strategize, and plan; and to refuse to caretake or nurture others. I was taught that it was not proper for a female to be violent, that it was "unnatural." My brother was taught that his value would be determined by his will to do violence (albeit in appropriate settings). He was taught that for a boy, enjoying violence was a good thing (albeit in appropriate settings). He was taught that a boy should not express feelings. I was taught that girls could and should express feelings, or at least some of them. When I responded with rage at being denied a toy, I was taught as a girl in a patriarchal household that rage was not an appropriate feminine feeling, that it should be not only not be expressed but be eradicated. When my brother responded with rage at being denied a toy, he was taught as a boy in a patriarchal household that his ability to express rage was good but that he had to learn the best setting to unleash his hostility. It was not good for him to use his rage to oppose the wishes of his parents, but later, when he grew up, he was taught that rage was permitted and that allowing rage to provoke him to violence would help him protect home and nation.

We lived in farm country, isolated from other people. Our sense of gender roles was learned from our parents, from the ways we saw them behave. My brother and I remember our confusion about gender. In reality I was stronger and more violent than my brother, which we learned quickly was bad. And he was a gentle, peaceful boy, which we learned was really bad. Although we were often confused, we knew one fact for certain: we could not be and act the way we wanted to, doing what we felt like. It was clear to us that our behavior had to follow a predetermined, gendered script. We both learned the word "patriarchy" in our adult life, when we learned that the script that had determined what we should be, the identities we should make, was based on patriarchal values and beliefs about gender.

I was always more interested in challenging patriarchy than my brother was because it was the system that was always leaving me out of things that I wanted to be part of. In our family life of the fifties, marbles were a boy's game. My brother had inherited his marbles from men in the family; he had a tin box to keep them in. All sizes and shapes, marvelously colored, they were to my eye the most beautiful objects. We played together with them, often with me aggressively clinging to the marble I liked best, refusing to share. When Dad was at work, our stay-at-home mom was quite content to see us playing marbles together. Yet Dad, looking at our play from a patriarchal perspective, was disturbed by what he saw. His daughter, aggressive and competitive, was a better player than his son. His son was passive; the boy did not really seem to care who won and was willing to give over marbles on demand. Dad decided that this play had to end, that both my brother and I needed to learn a lesson about appropriate gender roles.

One evening my brother was given permission by Dad to bring out the tin of marbles. I announced my desire to play and was told by my brother that "girls did not play with marbles," that it was a boy's game. This made no sense to my four- or five-year-old mind, and I insisted on my right to play by picking up marbles and shooting them. Dad intervened to tell me to stop. I did not listen. His voice grew louder and louder. Then suddenly he snatched me up, broke a board from our screen door, and began to beat me with it, telling me, "You're just a little girl. When I tell you to do something, I mean for you to do it." He beat me and he beat me, wanting me to acknowledge that I understood what I had done. His rage, his violence captured everyone's attention. Our family sat spellbound, rapt before the pornography of patriarchal violence. After this beating I was banished—forced to stay alone in the dark. Mama came into the bedroom to soothe the pain, telling me in her soft southern voice, "I tried to warn you. You need to accept that you are just a little girl and girls can't do what boys do." In service to patriarchy her task was to reinforce that Dad had done the right thing by putting me in my place, by restoring the natural social order.

I remember this traumatic event so well because it was a story told again and again within our family. No one cared that the constant retelling might trigger post-traumatic stress; the retelling was necessary to reinforce both the message and the remembered state of absolute powerlessness. The recollection of this brutal whipping of a little-girl daughter by a big strong man, served as more than just a reminder to me of my gendered place, it was a reminder to everyone watching/remembering, to all my siblings, male and female, and to our grown-woman mother that our patriarchal father was the ruler in our household. We were to remember that if we did not obey his rules, we would be punished, punished even unto death. This is the way we were experientially schooled in the art of patriarchy.

There is nothing unique or even exceptional about this experience. Listen to the voices of wounded grown children raised in patriarchal homes and you will hear different versions with the same underlying theme, the use of violence to reinforce our indoctrination and acceptance of patriarchy. In *How Can I Get Through to You?* family therapist

Terrence Real tells how his sons were initiated into patriarchal thinking even as their parents worked to create a loving home in which antipatriarchal values prevailed. He tells of how his young son Alexander enjoyed dressing as Barbie until boys playing with his older brother witnessed his Barbie persona and let him know by their gaze and their shocked, disapproving silence that his behavior was unacceptable:

> Without a shred of malevolence, the stare my son received transmitted a message. You are not to do this. And the medium that message was broadcast in was a potent emotion: shame. At three, Alexander was learning the rules. A ten-second wordless transaction was powerful enough to dissuade my son from that instant forward from what had been a favorite activity. I call such moments of induction the "normal traumatization" of boys.

To indoctrinate boys into the rules of patriarchy, we force them to feel pain and to deny their feelings.

My stories took place in the fifties; the stories Real tells are recent. They all underscore the tyranny of patriarchal thinking, the power of patriarchal culture to hold us captive. Real is one of the most enlightened thinkers on the subject of patriarchal masculinity in our nation, and yet he lets readers know that he is not able to keep his boys out of patriarchy's reach. They suffer its assaults, as do all boys and girls, to a greater or lesser degree. No doubt by creating a loving home that is not patriarchal, Real at least offers his boys a choice: they can choose to be themselves or they can choose conformity with patriarchal roles. Real uses the phrase "psychological patriarchy" to describe the patriarchal thinking common to females and males. Despite the contemporary visionary feminist thinking that makes clear that a patriarchal thinker need not be a male, most folks continue to see men as the problem of patriarchy. This is simply not the case. Women can be as wedded to patriarchal thinking and action as men.

Psychotherapist John Bradshaw's clear-sighted definition of patriarchy in *Creating Love* is a useful one: "The dictionary defines 'patriarchy' as a 'social organization marked by the supremacy of the father in the clan or family in both domestic and religious functions. . . .' Patriarchy is characterized by male domination and power." He states further that "patriarchal rules still govern most of the world's religious, school systems, and family systems." Describing the most damaging of these rules, Bradshaw lists "blind obedience—the foundation upon which patriarchy stands; the repression of all emotions except fear; the destruction of individual willpower; and the repression of thinking whenever it departs from the authority figure's way of thinking." Patriarchal thinking shapes the values of our culture. We are socialized into this system, females as well as males. Most of us learned patriarchal attitudes in our family of origin, and they were usually taught to us by our mothers. These attitudes were reinforced in schools and religious institutions.

The contemporary presence of female-headed households has led many people to assume that children in these households are not learning patriarchal values because no male is present. They assume that men are the sole teachers of patriarchal thinking. Yet many female-headed households endorse and promote patriarchal thinking with far greater passion than two-parent households. Because they do not have an experiential reality to challenge false fantasies of gender roles, women in such households are far more likely to idealize the patriarchal male role and patriarchal men than are women who live with patriarchal men every day. We need to highlight the role women play in perpetuating and sustaining patriarchal culture so that we will recognize patriarchy as a system women and men support equally, even if men receive more rewards from that system. Dismantling and changing patriarchal culture is work that men and women must do together.

Clearly we cannot dismantle a system as long as we engage in collective denial about its impact on our lives. Patriarchy requires male dominance by any means necessary, hence it supports, promotes, and condones sexist violence. We hear the most about sexist violence in public discourses about rape and abuse by domestic partners. But the most common forms of patriarchal violence are those that take place in the home between patriarchal parents and children. The point of such violence is usually to reinforce a dominator model, in which the authority figure is deemed ruler over those without power and given the right to maintain that rule through practices of subjugation, subordination, and submission.

Keeping males and females from telling the truth about what happens to them in families is one way patriarchal culture is maintained. A great majority of individuals enforce an unspoken rule in the culture as a whole that demands we keep the secrets of patriarchy, thereby protecting the rule of the father. This rule of silence is upheld when the culture refuses everyone easy access even to the word "patriarchy." Most children do not learn what to call this system of institutionalized gender roles, so rarely do we name it in everyday speech. This silence promotes denial. And how can we organize to challenge and change a system that cannot be named?

It is no accident that feminists began to use the word "patriarchy" to replace the more commonly used "male chauvanism" and "sexism." These courageous voices wanted men and women to become more aware of the way patriarchy affects us all. In popular culture the word itself was hardly used during the heyday of contemporary feminism. Antimale activists were no more eager than their sexist male counterparts to emphasize the system of patriarchy and the way it works. For to do so would have automatically exposed the notion that men were all-powerful and women powerless, that all men were oppressive and women always and only victims. By placing the blame for the perpetuation of sexism solely on men, these women could maintain their own allegiance to patriarchy, their own lust for power. They masked their longing to be dominators by taking on the mantle of victimhood.

Like many visionary radical feminists I challenged the misguided notion, put forward by women who were simply fed up with male exploitation and oppression, that men were "the enemy." As early as 1984 I included a chapter with the title "Men: Comrades in Struggle" in my book *Feminist Theory: From Margin to Center* urging advocates of feminist politics to challenge any rhetoric which placed the sole blame for perpetuating patriarchy and male domination onto men:

> Separatist ideology encourages women to ignore the negative impact of sexism on male personhood. It stresses polarization between the sexes. According to Joy Justice, separatists believe that there are "two basic perspectives" on the issue of naming the victims of sexism: "There is the perspective that men oppress women. And there is the perspective that people are people, and we are all hurt by rigid sex roles." . . . Both perspectives accurately describe our predicament. Men do oppress women. People are hurt by rigid sexist role patterns. These two realities coexist. Male oppression of women cannot be excused by the recognition that there are ways men are hurt by rigid sexist roles. Feminist activists should acknowledge that hurt, and work to change it—it exists. It does not erase or lessen male responsibility for supporting and perpetuating their power under patriarchy to exploit and oppress women in a manner far more grievous than the serious psychological stress and emotional pain caused by male conformity to rigid sexist role patterns.

Throughout this essay I stressed that feminist advocates collude in the pain of men wounded by patriarchy when they falsely represent men as always and only powerful, as always and only gaining privileges from their blind obedience to patriarchy. I emphasized that patriarchal ideology brainwashes men to believe that their domination of women is beneficial when it is not:

> Often feminist activists affirm this logic when we should be constantly naming these acts as expressions of perverted power relations, general lack of control of one's actions, emotional powerlessness, extreme irrationality, and in many cases, outright insanity. Passive male absorption of sexist ideology enables men to falsely interpret this disturbed behavior positively. As long as men are brainwashed to equate violent domination and abuse of women with privilege, they will have no understanding of the damage done to themselves or to others, and no motivation to change.

Patriarchy demands of men that they become and remain emotional cripples. Since it is a system that denies men full access to their freedom of will, it is difficult for any man of any class to rebel against patriarchy, to be disloyal to the patriarchal parent, be that parent female or male.

The man who has been my primary bond for more than twelve years was traumatized by the patriarchal dynamics in his family of origin. When I met him he was in his twenties. While his formative years had been spent in the company of a violent, alcoholic dad, his circumstances changed when he was twelve and he began to live alone with his mother. In the early years of our relationship he talked openly about his hostility and rage toward his abusing dad. He was not interested in forgiving him or understanding the circumstances that had shaped and influenced his dad's life, either in his childhood or in his working life as a military man.

In the early years of our relationship he was extremely critical of male domination of women and children. Although he did not use the word "patriarchy," he understood its meaning and he opposed it. His gentle, quiet manner often led folks to ignore him, counting him among the weak and the powerless. By the age of thirty he began to assume a more macho persona, embracing the dominator model that he had once critiqued. Donning the mantle of patriarch, he gained greater respect and visibility. More women were drawn to him. He was noticed more in public spheres. His criticism of male domination ceased. And indeed he begin to mouth patriarchal rhetoric, saying the kind of sexist stuff that would have appalled him in the past.

These changes in his thinking and behavior were triggered by his desire to be accepted and affirmed in a patriarchal workplace and rationalized by his desire to get ahead. His story is not unusual. Boys brutalized and victimized by patriarchy more often than not become patriarchal, embodying the abusive patriarchal masculinity that they once clearly recognized as evil. Few men brutally abused as boys in the name of patriarchal maleness courageously resist the brainwashing and remain true to themselves. Most males conform to patriarchy in one way or another.

Indeed, radical feminist critique of patriarchy has practically been silenced in our culture. It has become a subcultural discourse available only to well-educated elites. Even in those circles, using the word "patriarchy" is regarded as passé. Often in my lectures when I use the phrase "imperialist white-supremacist capitalist patriarchy" to describe our nation's political system, audiences laugh. No one has ever explained why accurately naming this system is funny. The laughter is itself a weapon of patriarchal terrorism. It functions as a disclaimer, discounting the significance of what is being named. It suggests that the words themselves are problematic and not the system they describe. I interpret this laughter as the audience's way of showing discomfort with being asked to ally themselves with an antipatriarchal disobedient critique. This laughter reminds me that if I dare to challenge patriarchy openly, I risk not being taken seriously.

Citizens in this nation fear challenging patriarchy even as they lack overt awareness that they are fearful, so deeply embedded in our collective unconscious are the rules of patriarchy. I often tell audiences that if we were to go door-to-door asking if we should end male violence against women, most people would give their unequivocal support. Then if you told them we can only stop male violence against women by ending male domination, by eradicating patriarchy, they would begin to hesitate, to change their position. Despite the many gains of contemporary feminist movement—greater equality for women in the workforce, more tolerance for the relinquishing of rigid gender roles—patriarchy as a system remains intact, and many people continue to believe that it is needed if humans are to survive as a species. This belief seems ironic, given that patriarchal methods of organizing nations, especially the insistence on violence as a means of social control, has actually led to the slaughter of millions of people on the planet.

Until we can collectively acknowledge the damage patriarchy causes and the suffering it creates, we cannot address male pain. We cannot demand for men the right to be whole, to be givers and sustainers of life. Obviously some patriarchal men are reliable and even benevolent caretakers and providers, but still they are imprisoned by a system that undermines their mental health.

Patriarchy promotes insanity. It is at the root of the psychological ills troubling men in our nation. Nevertheless there is no mass concern for the plight of men. In *Stiffed: The Betrayal of the American Man,* Susan Faludi includes very little discussion of patriarchy:

> Ask feminists to diagnose men's problems and you will often get a very clear explanation: men are in crisis because women are properly challenging male dominance. Women are asking men to share the public reins and men can't bear it. Ask antifeminists and you will get a diagnosis that is, in one respect, similar. Men are troubled, many conservative pundits say, because women have gone far beyond their demands for equal treatment and are now trying to take power and control away from men. . . . The underlying message: men cannot be men, only eunuchs, if they are not in control. Both the feminist and antifeminist views are rooted in a peculiarly modern American perception that to

> be a man means to be at the controls and at all times to feel yourself in control.

Faludi never interrogates the notion of control. She never considers that the notion that men were somehow in control, in power, and satisfied with their lives before contemporary feminist movement is false.

Patriarchy as a system has denied males access to full emotional well-being, which is not the same as feeling rewarded, successful, or powerful because of one's capacity to assert control over others. To truly address male pain and male crisis we must as a nation be willing to expose the harsh reality that patriarchy has damaged men in the past and continues to damage them in the present. If patriarchy were truly rewarding to men, the violence and addiction in family life that is so all-pervasive would not exist. This violence was not created by feminism. If patriarchy were rewarding, the overwhelming dissatisfaction most men feel in their work lives—a dissatisfaction extensively documented in the work of Studs Terkel and echoed in Faludi's treatise—would not exist.

In many ways *Stiffed* was yet another betrayal of American men because Faludi spends so much time trying not to challenge patriarchy that she fails to highlight the necessity of ending patriarchy if we are to liberate men. Rather she writes:

> Instead of wondering why men resist women's struggle for a freer and healthier life, I began to wonder why men refrain from engaging in their own struggle. Why, despite a crescendo of ran-

> dom tantrums, have they offered no methodical, reasoned response to their predicament: Given the untenable and insulting nature of the demands placed on men to prove themselves in our culture, why don't men revolt? . . . Why haven't men responded to the series of betrayals in their own lives—to the failures of their fathers to make good on their promises—with something coequal to feminism?

Note that Faludi does not dare risk either the ire of feminist females by suggesting that men can find salvation in feminist movement or rejection by potential male readers who are solidly antifeminist by suggesting that they have something to gain from engaging feminism.

So far in our nation visionary feminist movement is the only struggle for justice that emphasizes the need to end patriarchy. No mass body of women has challenged patriarchy and neither has any group of men come together to lead the struggle. The crisis facing men is not the crisis of masculinity, it is the crisis of patriarchal masculinity. Until we make this distinction clear, men will continue to fear that any critique of patriarchy represents a threat. Distinguishing political patriarchy, which he sees as largely committed to ending sexism, therapist Terrence Real makes clear that the patriarchy damaging us all is embedded in our psyches:

> Psychological patriarchy is the dynamic between those qualities deemed "masculine" and "feminine" in which half of our human

> traits are exalted while the other half is devalued. Both men and women participate in this tortured value system. Psychological patriarchy is a "dance of contempt," a perverse form of connection that replaces true intimacy with complex, covert layers of dominance and submission, collusion and manipulation. It is the unacknowledged paradigm of relationships that has suffused Western civilization generation after generation, deforming both sexes, and destroying the passionate bond between them.

By highlighting psychological patriarchy, we see that everyone is implicated and we are freed from the misperception that men are the enemy. To end patriarchy we must challenge both its psychological and its concrete manifestations in daily life. There are folks who are able to critique patriarchy but unable to act in an antipatriarchal manner.

To end male pain, to respond effectively to male crisis, we have to name the problem. We have to both acknowledge that the problem is patriarchy and work to end patriarchy. Terrence Real offers this valuable insight: "The reclamation of wholeness is a process even more fraught for men than it has been for women, more difficult and more profoundly threatening to the culture at large." If men are to reclaim the essential goodness of male being, if they are to regain the space of openheartedness and emotional expressiveness that is the foundation of well-being, we must envision alternatives to patriarchal masculinity. We must all change.

3

Being a Boy

Boys are not seen as lovable in patriarchal culture. Even though sexism has always decreed that boy children have more status than girls, status and even the rewards of privilege are not the same as being loved. Patriarchal assault on the emotional life of boys begins at the moment of their birth. Contrary to sexist mythology, in the real world of male and female babies, male babies express themselves more. They cry longer and louder. They come into the world wanting to be seen and heard. Sexist thinking at its worst leads many parents to let male infants cry without a comforting touch because they fear that holding baby boys too much, comforting them too much, might cause them to grow up wimpy. Thankfully, there has been enough of a break with rigid sexist roles to allow aware parents to reject this faulty logic and give boy babies the same comfort that they give or would give girls.

In recent years it has become clear to researchers working on promoting the emotional life of boys that patriarchal culture influences parents to devalue the emotional development of boys. Naturally this disregard affects boys' capacity to love and be loving. Dan Kindlon and Michael Thompson, authors of *Raising Cain: Protecting the Emotional*

Life of Boys, stress that their research shows that boys are free to be more emotional in early childhood because they have not yet learned to fear and despise expressing dependence: "Every child, boys included, comes into this world wanting to love and be loved by his parents. Forty years of research on emotional attachment shows that without it children die or suffer severe emotional damage." Despite these powerful insights they do not talk about the impact of patriarchy. They do not tell readers that to truly protect the emotional life of boys, we must tell the truth about the power of patriarchy. We must dare to face the way in which patriarchal thinking blinds everyone so that we cannot see that the emotional lives of boys cannot be fully honored as long as notions of patriarchal masculinity prevail. We cannot teach boys that "real men" either do not feel or do not express feelings, then expect boys to feel comfortable getting in touch with their feelings.

Much of the traditional research on the emotional life of boys draws the connection between notions of male dominance and the shutting down of emotions in boyhood even as the researchers act as though patriarchal values can remain intact. Popular bestselling books such as *Raising Cain* and James Garbarino's *Lost Boys: Why Our Sons Turn Violent and How We can Save Them* outline the way boys are being emotionally damaged, but they fail to offer a courageous alternative vision, one that would fundamentally challenge patriarchal masculinity. Instead these books imply that within the existing patriarchal system, boyhood should be free of patriarchal demands. The value of patriarchy itself is never addressed. In *Raising Cain* the authors conclude by contending: "What boys need, first and foremost, is to be seen through a different lens than tradition prescribes. Individually, and as a culture, we must discard the distorted view of boys that ignores or denies their capacity for feelings, the view that colors even boys' perception of themselves as above or outside a life of emotions." Kindlon and Thompson carefully depoliticize their language. Their use of the word "tradition" belies the reality that the patriarchal culture which has socialized almost everyone in our nation to dismiss the emotional life of boys is an entrenched social and political system. Nor is it an accident of nature. Antifeminist women like Christina Hoff Sommers curry patriarchal favor with men by spreading the idea, put forward in Sommers's book *The War against Boys,* that "feminism is harming our young men." Sommers falsely assumes that educating boys to be antipatriarchal is "resocializing boys in the direction of femininity." Conveniently, she ignores that feminist thinkers are as critical of sexist notions of femininity as we are of patriarchal notions of masculinity. It is patriarchy, in its denial of the full humanity of boys, that threatens the emotional lives of boys, not feminist thinking. To change patriarchal "traditions" we must end patriarchy, in part by envisoning alternative ways of thinking about maleness, not only boyhood.

Without ever using the word "patriarchy" (he uses the phrase "traditional masculinity"), psychologist James Garbarino does suggest in *Lost Boys* that the cultivation of an androgynous selfhood, one that combines the traits deemed masculine and feminine, would affirm for boys their right to be emotional. In his section on "What Boys Need" Garbarino writes:

> Where and how do boys learn what it means to be a man? They seem to learn it all too often from the mass media and from the most visible males in their community, particularly their peers. Boys' friends are the arbitrators of what is masculine and what is feminine, so resilience among the boys in a community depends upon changing macho attitudes among male peer groups and broadening their concept of what a real man is and does.

Garbarino's is a powerful work, very much on target in the descriptions and information it offers about all the ways boys are traumatized by the demand that they deny their emotions. But it is also a disturbing one because the author himself seems unwilling to connect his recognition of the damage done to boys with a critique of patriarchal thinking and practice. It is as if he believes that somehow all that is needed is a revamping of patriarchal values so that boys' emotions can be supported, at least until the boys grow up.

Frankly, it is difficult to understand why these men who know so much about the way patriarchal thinking damages boys are unable to call the problem by its true name and by so doing free themselves to envision a world where the feelings of boys can really matter. Perhaps they are silent because any critique of patriarchy necessarily leads to a discussion of whether conversion to feminist thinking and practice is the answer. It has been hard for many male thinkers about the emotional life of boys to see feminism as a helpful theory because to a grave extent antimale sentiments among some feminists have led the movement to focus very little attention on the development of boys.

One of the tremendous failings of feminist theory and practice has been the lack of a concentrated study of boyhood, one that offers guidelines and strategies for alternative masculinity and ways of thinking about maleness. Indeed the feminist rhetoric that insisted on identifying males as the enemy often closed down the space where boys could be considered, where they could be deemed as worthy of rescue from patriarchal exploitation and oppression as were their female counterparts. Like the researchers who write about the emotional lives of boys from a nonfeminist perspective, feminist researchers are often unwilling or reluctant to target patriarchal thinking. Family therapist Olga Silverstein in *The Courage to Raise Good Men* says little about patriarchy even as she does offer alternative strategies for raising boys. There are two major barriers preventing researchers from targeting patriarchy. Researchers fear that overtly political analysis will alienate readers on one hand, and on the other hand they may simply have no alternative visions to offer.

Feminist theory has offered us brilliant critiques of patriarchy and very few insightful ideas about alternative masculinity, especially in relation to boys. Many feminist women who birthed boys found themselves reluctant to challenge conventional aspects of patriarchal masculinity when their boys wanted to embrace those values. They found they did not want to deny their sons access to toy guns or to tell them to just be passive when another boy was attacking them on the playground. For many enlightened, single-parent feminist mothers with limited economic resources, the effort to consistently map for their sons alternatives to patriarchal masculinity simply takes too much time.

One of my very best friends is a single mother with two children, an older daughter and a younger son. When her son was born I suggested we name him Ruby. His biological dad jokingly made the point that "she should have her own son and name him Ruby." Well, his middle name is Ruby. When he was around the age of five he decided he wanted to use the name Ruby. The boys at school let him know through teasing that this was a girl's name. As an intervention he and his mom brought to school pictures of all the men through history named Ruby. Then later on he wanted to paint his nails with fingernail polish and wear it to school. Again the boys let him know that boys do not use nail polish. His mother and sister gathered all the "cool" adult guys knew they to come to school and show that males can use nail polish. These were my friend's graduate student years, however; when she began working full-time, such vigilance became harder to maintain. Just recently her son told her how much he likes the way she smells. She shared with him that he could smell the same. He let her know that there was no way he could go to school smelling sweet. He had gotten the message that "boys don't smell good." Instead of urging him to rise to the latest challenge, she now allows him to choose and does not judge his choice. Yet she feels sad for him, sad that conformity to patriarchal standards interfered with his longings.

Many antipatriarchal parents find that the alternative masculinities they support for their boy children are shattered not by grown-ups but by sexist male peers. Progressive parents who strive to be vigilant about the mass media their boys have access to must constantly intervene and offer teachings to counter the patriarchal pedagogy that is deemed "normal." *In How Can I Get Through to You?* Terrrence Real, father of two sons, states:

> Our sons learn the code early and well, don't cry, don't be vulnerable; don't show weakness—ultimately, don't show that you care. As a society, we may have some notion that raising whole boys and girls is a good idea, but that doesn't mean that we actually do. Even though you or I might be committed to raising less straitjacketed kids, the culture at large, while perhaps changing, is still far from changed. Try as we might, in movie theaters, classrooms, playgrounds our sons and daughters are bombarded with traditional messages about masculinity and femininity, hour by hour, day by day.

Again, Real uses the word "traditional" rather than "patriarchal." Yet traditions are rarely hard to change. What has been all but impossible to change is widespread cultural patriarchal propaganda. Yet we begin to protect the emotional well-being of boys and of all males when we call this propaganda by its true name, when we acknowledge that patriarchal culture requires that boys deny, suppress, and if all goes well, shut down their emotional awareness and their capacity to feel.

Little boys are the only males in our culture who are allowed to be fully, wholly in touch with their feelings, allowed moments when they can express without shame their desire to love and be loved. If they are very, very lucky, they are able to remain connected to their inner selves or some part of their inner selves before they enter a patriarchal school system where rigid sex roles will be enforced by peers as rigorously as they are in any adult male prison. Those rare boys who happen to live in antipatriarchal homes learn early to lead a double life: at home they can feel and express and be; outside the home they must conform to the role of patriarchal boy. Patriarchal boys, like their adult counterparts, know the rules: they know they must not express feelings, with the exception of anger; that they must not do anything considered feminine or womanly. A national survey of adolescent males revealed their passive acceptance of patriarchal masculinity. Researchers found that boys agreed that to be truly manly, they must command respect, be tough, not talk about problems, and dominate females.

Every day across this country boys consume mass media images that send them one message about how to deal with emotions, and that message is "Act out." Usually acting out means aggression directed outward. Kicking, screaming, and hitting get attention. Since patriarchal parenting does not teach boys to express their feelings in words, either boys act out or they implode. Very few boys are taught to express with words what they feel, when they feel it. And even when boys are able to express feelings in early childhood, they learn as they grow up that they are not supposed to feel and they shut down.

The confusion boys experience about their identity is heightened during adolescence. In many ways the fact that today's boy often has a wider range of emotional expression in early childhood but is forced to suppress emotional awareness later on makes adolescence all the more stressful for boys. Tragically, were it not for the extreme violence that has erupted among teenage boys throughout our nation, the emotional life of boys would still be ignored. Although therapists tell us that mass media images of male violence and dominance teach boys that violence is alluring and satisfying, when individual boys are violent, especially when they murder randomly, pundits tend to behave as though it were a mystery why boys are so violent.

Progressive feminist research on adolescent males has debunked the heretofore accepted notion that it is natural for boys to go through an antisocial stage where they disassociate and disconnect. Recent studies indicate that it is actually emotionally damaging to young males to be isolated and without emotional care or nurturance. In the past it was assumed that aggression was part of the ritual of separation, a means for the growing boy to assert his autonomy. Yet clearly, just as girls learn how to be autonomous and how to create healthy distance from parents without becoming antisocial, boys can do the same. In healthy families boys are able to learn and assert autonomy without engaging in antisocial behavior, without isolating themselves. All over the world terrorist regimes use isolation to break people's spirit. This weapon of psychological terrorism is daily deployed in our nation against teenage boys. In isolation they lose the sense of their value and worth. No wonder then that when they reenter a community, they bring with them killing rage as their primary defense.

Even though masses of American boys will not commit violent crimes resulting in murder, the truth that no one wants to name is that all boys are being raised to be killers even if they learn to hide the killer within and act as benevolent young patriarchs. (More and more girls who embrace patriarchal thinking also embrace the notion that they must be violent to have power.) Talking to teenage girls of all classes who are being secretly hit or beaten by boyfriends (who say that they are "disciplining" them), one hears the same Dr. Jekyll and Mr. Hyde narratives that grown women tell when talking about their relationships with abusive men. These girls describe seemingly nice guys who have rageful outbursts. Time and time again we hear on our national news about the seemingly kind, quiet young male whose violent underpinnings are suddenly revealed. Boys are encouraged by patriarchal thinking to claim rage as the easiest path to manliness. It should come as no surprise, then, that beneath the surface there is a seething anger in boys, a rage waiting for the moment to be heard.

Much of the anger boys express is itself a response to the demand that they not show any other emotions. Anger feels better than numbness because it often leads to more instrumental action. Anger can be, and usually is, the hiding place for fear and pain. In *The Heart of the Soul* authors Gary Zukav and Linda Francis explore the ways anger barricades the feeling self:

> Anger prevents love and isolates the one who is angry. It is an attempt, often successful, to push away what is most longed for—companionship and understanding. It is a denial of the humanness of others, as well as a denial of your

> own humanness. Anger is the agony of believing that you are not capable of being understood, and that you are not worthy of being understood. It is a wall that separates you from others as effectively as if it were concrete, thick, and very high. There is no way through it, under it, or over it.

Certainly in almost all the situations where boys have killed, we discover narratives of rage that describe the emotional realities before they happen. Importantly, this anger is expressed cross a broad spectrum of class, race, and family circumstance. Violent boys from affluent homes often are as emotionally alienated as their ghetto counterparts.

At a time in our nation's history when more boys than ever are being raised in single-parent, female-headed homes, mass media send the message that a single mother is unfit to raise a healthy boy child. All over our nation mothers worry that their parenting may be damaging their sons. This is the issue Olga Silverstein tackles head-on in *The Courage to Raise Good Men.* Commenting that many people still believe that mothers compromise their sons' masculinity, she writes: "Most women, like most men, feel that a mother's influence will ultimately be harmful to a male child, that it will weaken him and that only the example of a man can lead a son into manhood. Single mothers in particular are haunted by the dread of producing a sissy." Homophobia underlies the fear that allowing boys to feel will turn them gay; this fear is often most intense in single-parent homes. As a consequence mothers in these families may be overly harsh and profoundly emotionally withholding with their sons, believing that this treatment will help the boys to be more masculine.

No matter that information abounds that lets the public know that many gay males come from two-parent homes and can be macho and woman-hating, misguided assumptions about what makes a male gay still flourish. Every day boys who express feelings are psychologically terrorized, and in extreme cases brutally beaten, by parents who fear that a man of feeling must be homosexual. Gay men share with straight men the same notions about acceptable masculinity. Luckily there have been and are individual gay men who dare to challenge patriarchal masculinity. However, most gay men in our culture are as embracing of sexist thinking as are heterosexuals. Their patriarchal thinking leads them to construct paradigms of desirable sexual behavior that is similar to that of patriarchal straight men. Hence many gay men are as angry as their straight counterparts.

Just as maternal sadism flourishes in a world where women are made to feel that their emotional cruelty to sons makes them better prepared for manhood, paternal sadism is the natural outcome of patriarchal values. In the book *The Man I Might Become: Gay Men Write about Their Fathers,* edited by Bruce Shenitz, many of the stories of boyhood describe rituals of paternal sadism. As James Saslow writes in "Daddy Was a Hot Number":

> All children suffer that aching stab of inadequacy when Papa turns his face away; it's just twice as sharp when he's your object of desire as well as your mentor and role model. Only mother

> love is unconditional. . . . But fatherly love is also about licking the child into shape. . . . Fathers challenge and then judge us—their role in socializing the next generation. In this mythic battle of wills, persuasion and example are the preferred weapons, but if they don't work, the drill sergeant will have to unleash the A-bomb of familial warfare: rejection.

Most patriarchal fathers in our nation do not use physical violence to keep their sons in check; they use various techniques of psychological terrorism, the primary one being the practice of shaming. Patriarchal fathers cannot love their sons because the rules of patriarchy dictate that they stand in competition with their sons, ready to prove that they are the real man, the one in charge. In his essay "Finding the Light and Keeping It in Front of Me," Bob Vance describes walking behind his father as a boy longing to connect but knowing intuitively that no connection was possible: "Something inhibits me from asking him for what I need. I know, if a very young boy can intuit such things, that I am left out of his world and am somehow forbidden to ask him what I can do to have him take me into his world, to hold me playfully or tenderly. The rift begins here. This is the earliest memory I have of my father."

To the patriarchal dad, sons can only be regarded as recruits in training, hence they must constantly be subjected to sadomasochistic power struggles designed to toughen them up, to prepare them to maintain the patriarchal legacy. As sons they inhabit a world where fathers strive to keep them in the one-down position; as patriarchs in training they must learn how to assume a one-up role. Real explains:

> Sustaining relationships with others requires a good relationship to ourselves. Healthy self-esteem is an internal sense of worth, that pulls one neither into "better than" grandiosity nor "less than" shame. . . . Contempt is why so many men have such trouble staying connected. Since healthy self-esteem—being neither one up nor down—is not yet a real option, and since riding in the one-down position elicits disdain, in oneself and in others, most men learn to hide the chronic shame that dogs them . . . running from their own humanity and from closeness to anyone else along with it.

This flight from closeness is most intense in the lives of adolescent boys because in that liminal zone between childhood and young adulthood they are experiencing a range of emotions that leave them feeling out of control, fearful that they will not measure up to the standards of patriarchal masculinity. Suppressed rage is the perfect hiding place for all these fears.

Despite major changes in gender roles in public life, in private many boys are traumatized by relationships with distant or absent fathers. Working with groups of men, listening as they talk about boyhood, I hear the stories they tell about their fathers' lack of emotional connection. As they attempt to measure up to patriarchal expectations, many boys fear the wrath of the father. In *Man Enough:*

Fathers, Sons, and the Search for Masculinity, Frank Pittman recalls: "Fearing I didn't have enough of it, I was in awe of masculinity. I thought my father had some magical power he wasn't passing on to me, a secret he hadn't told me." Again and again the same assumption appears, which suggests that there exists a masculine ideal that young males are not sure how to attain and that undermines their self-esteem. And the crisis of this longing seems most deeply felt by boys with absent fathers. Without a positive connection to a real adult man, they are far more likely to invest in a hypermasculine patriarchal ideal. Fear of not being able to attain the right degree of manliness is often translated into rage. Many teenage boys are angry because the fantasy emotional connection between father and son, the love that they imagine will be there, is never realized. In its place there is just a space of empty longing. Even when it becomes evident that the fantasy will not be fulfilled, that the "father wound" will not be healed, boys hold on to the longing. It may give them a sense of quest and purpose to feel they will someday find the father or, through having children, become the father they dream about.

Frustrated in their quest for father bonding, boys often feel tremendous sorrow and depression. They can mask these feelings because they are allowed to isolate themselves, to turn away from the world and escape into music, television, video games, etc. There is no emotional outlet for the grief of the disappointed teenage boy. Being able to mourn the loss of emotional connection with his father would be a healthy way to cope with disappointment. But boys have no space to mourn. This need for a space to grieve is poignantly portrayed in the film *Life as a House.* Learning that he has cancer and only a short time to live, the father in the film seeks to connect with his sexually confused, angry, drug-using teenage son, who lives with his mother and stepfather. In the short time he lives with his dad, the son is able to develop an emotional connection. When the son finds out that his dad is dying, he rages about being offered love that is not going to last. In Donald Dutton's study of abusive men, *The Batterer*, he observes that there are few male models for grieving, and he emphasizes that "men in particular seem incapable of grieving and mourning on an individual basis. Trapped by a world that tells them boys should not express feelings, teenage males have nowhere to go where grief is accepted." As much as grown-ups complain about adolescent male anger, most adults are more comfortable confronting a raging teenager than one who is overwhelmed by sorrow and cannot stop weeping. Boys learn to cover up grief with anger; the more troubled the boy, the more intense the mask of indifference. Shutting down emotionally is the best defense when the longing for connection must be denied.

Teenagers are the most unloved group in our nation. Teenagers are often feared precisely because they are often exposing the hypocrisy of parents and of the world around them. And no group of teenagers is more feared than a pack of teenage boys. Emotionally abandoned by parents and by society as a whole, many boys are angry, but no one really cares about this anger unless it leads to violent behavior. If boys take their rage and sit in front of a computer all day, never speaking, never relating, no one cares. If boys take their rage to the mall, no one cares, as long as it is contained. In *Lost Boys* therapist James Garbarino testifies that when it comes to boys, "neglect is more common than abuse: more kids are emotionally abandoned than are directly attacked, physically or emotionally." Emotional neglect lays the groundwork for the emotional numbing that helps boys feel better about being cut off. Eruptions of rage in boys are most often deemed normal, explained by the age-old justification for adolescent patriarchal misbehavior, "Boys will be boys." Patriarchy both creates the rage in boys and then contains it for later use, making it a resource to exploit later on as boys become men. As a national product, this rage can be garnered to further imperialism, hatred, and oppression of women and men globally. This rage is needed if boys are to become men willing to travel around the world to fight wars without ever demanding that other ways of solving conflict be found.

Ever since masses of American boys began, in the wake of the civil rights struggle, sexual liberation, and feminist movement, to demand their right to be psychologically whole and expressed those demands most visibly by refusing to fight in the Vietnam War, mass media as a propaganda tool for imperialist white-supremacist capitalist patriarchy have targeted young males and engaged in heavy-handed brainwashing to reinforce psychological patriarchy. Today small boys and young men are daily inundated with a poisonous pedagogy that supports male violence and male domination, that teaches boys that unchecked violence is acceptable, that teaches them to disrespect and hate women. Given this reality and the concomitant emotional abandonment of boys, it should surprise no one that boys are violent, that they are willing to kill; it should surprise us that the killing is not yet widespread.

Ruthless patriarchal assault on the self-esteem of teenage boys has become an accepted norm. There is a grave silence about adult male tyranny in relation to teenage boys. Much of the adult male terrorism of and competition with little boys and young males is conducted through mass media. Much of the mass media directed at young male consumers is created by self-hating, emotionally shut-down adult men who have only the pornography of violence to share with younger men. To that end they create images that make killing alluring and the sexual exploitation of females the seductive reward. In the wake of feminist, antiracist, and postcolonial critiques of imperialist white-supremacist capitalist patriarchy, the backlash that aims to reinscribe patriarchy is fierce. While feminism may ignore boys and young males, capitalist patriarchal men do not. It was adult, white, wealthy males in this country who first read and fell in love with the *Harry Potter* books. Though written by a British female, initially described by the rich white American men who "discovered" her as a working-class single mom, J. K. Rowling's *Harry Potter* books are clever modern reworkings of the English schoolboy novel. Harry as our modern-day hero is the supersmart, gifted, blessed, white boy genius (a mini patriarch) who "rules" over the equally smart kids, including an occasional girl and an occasional male of color. But these books also glorify war, depicted as killing on behalf of the "good."

The *Harry Potter* movies glorify the use of violence to maintain control over others. In *Harry Potter: The Chamber of Secrets* violence when used by the acceptable groups is deemed positive. Sexism and racist thinking in the *Harry Potter* books are rarely critiqued. Had the author been a ruling-class white male, feminist thinkers might have been more active in challenging the imperialism, racism, and sexism of Rowling's books.

Again and again I hear parents, particularly antipatriarchal parents, express concern about the contents of these books while praising them for drawing more boys to reading. Of course American children were bombarded with an advertising blitz telling them that they should read these books. *Harry Potter* began as national news sanctioned by mass media. Books that do not reinscribe patriarchal masculinity do not get the approval the *Harry Potter* books have received. And children rarely have an opportunity to know that any books exist which offer an alternative to patriarchal masculinist visions. The phenomenal financial success of *Harry Potter* means that boys will henceforth have an array of literary clones to choose from.

Literature for children is just as fixated on furthering patriarchal attitudes as television. There are just few a books with male characters focusing on boys that challenge the patriarchal norm in anyway. Since these books do not abound there is no way to know what impact they might have in teaching boys alternative masculinities. Writing a series of children's book for boys, I was initially amazed by how difficult it was for me, a visionary feminist theorist, to imagine new images and texts for boys. Shopping for books for my nephew first alerted me to the absence of progressive literature for boys. In my first children's book with male characters, *Be Boy Buzz,* I wanted to celebrate boyhood without reinscribing patriarchal norms. I wanted to write a text that would just express love for boys. It is a book aimed at little boys. This book strives to honor the holistic well-being of boys and to express love of them whether they are laughing, acting out, or just sitting still. The books I have written are aimed at offering boys ways to cope with their emotional selves. The point is to stimulate in boys emotional awareness and to affirm that awareness.

To truly protect and honor the emotional lives of boys we must challenge patriarchal culture. And until that culture changes, we must create the subcultures, the sanctuaries where boys can learn to be who they are uniquely, without being forced to conform to patriarchal masculine visions. To love boys rightly we must value their inner lives enough to construct worlds, both private and public, where their right to wholeness can be consistently celebrated and affirmed, where their need to love and be loved can be fulfilled.

4

Stopping Male Violence

Every day in America men are violent. Their violence is deemed "natural" by the psychology of patriarchy, which insists that there is a biological connection between having a penis and the will to do violence. This thinking continues to shape notions of manhood in our society despite the fact that it has been documented that cultures exist in the world where men are not violent in everyday life, where rape and murder are rare occurrences. Every day in our nation there are men who turn away from violence. These men do not write books about how they manage to navigate the terrain of patriarchal masculinity without succumbing to the lure of violence. As women have gained the right to be patriarchal men in drag, women are engaging in acts of violence similar to those of their male counterparts. This serves to remind us that the will to use violence is really not linked to biology but to a set of expectations about the nature of power in a dominator culture.

Over the decades no matter how many television shows and movies we have watched in which the hero is the good man who uses violence to win the fight with bad men, many people have long felt that feminist thinkers exaggerate the degree to which men are violent in their daily lives.

Radical feminist Andrea Dworkin has courageously and consistently dared to name the widespread scope of male violence against women. In *Scapegoat* she writes: "A recent United Nations report says that 'violence against women is the world's most pervasive form of human rights abuse.' In the United States the Justice Department says that 'one out of twelve women will be stalked at some point in her lifetime.' The American Medical Association concluded that 'sexual assault and family violence are devastating the United States physical and emotional well-being;' in 1995 the AMA reported that 'more than 700,000 women in the United States are sexually assaulted each year, or one every 45 seconds.'" These facts address actual physical assault and do not cover the widespread emotional abuse that has practically become an accepted norm in male-female relationships whether between husband and wife, father and daughter, brother and sister, or girlfriend and boyfriend.

In *How Can I Get Through to You?* Terrence Real includes a chapter titled "A Conspiracy of Silence," in which he emphasizes that we are not allowed in this culture to speak the truth about what relationships with men are really like. This silence represents our collective cultural collusion with patriarchy. To be true to patriarchy we are all taught that we must keep men's secrets. Real points out that the fundamental secret we share is that we will remain silent: "When girls are inducted into womanhood, what is it exactly that they have to say that must be silenced. What is the truth women carry that cannot be spoken. The answer is simple and chilling. Girls, women—and also young boys—all share this in common. None may speak the truth about men." One of the truths that cannot be spoken is the daily violence enacted by men of all classes and races in our society—the violence of emotional abuse. In her groundbreaking work *Emotional Abuse* Marti Tamm Loring explains that emotional abuse is "an ongoing process in which one individual systematically diminishes and destroys the inner self of another. The essential ideas, feelings, perception, and personality characteristics of the victim are constantly belittled. . . . The most salient identifying characteristic of emotional abuse is its patterned aspect. . . . It is . . . the ongoing effort to demean and control, that constitutes emotional abuse." Significantly, emotional abuse in families is not just a component of the couple bond; it can determine the way everyone in a family relates. If a woman is patriarchal, it can be present in a single-parent home with no adult males present. In many homes patriarchal power resides with teenage boys who are abusive to single-parent moms; this is male violence against women.

When Real breaks the silence, the stories he shares are from family therapy sessions where clients openly reveal the way fathers have enacted rituals of power, using shaming, withdrawal, threats, and if all else fails, physical violence to maintain their position of dominance. In my family of origin our dad in a booming, angry voice would often scream repeatedly at Mom, "I will kill you." For years my nightmares were filled with an angry father sometimes killing Mom, sometimes killing me for trying to protect Mom. In our family, Dad was not consistently enraged, but the intense emotional and physical abuse that he unleashed on those rare occasions when he did act out violently kept everyone in check, living on the edge, living in fear. Usually a cold, silent, reserved man, Dad found his voice when speaking in anger.

The two men I have had as my primary relational bonds in my adult life are both quiet and reserved like my dad and my beloved grandfather. Unlike my grandfather, whom I never witnessed expressing anger, much less rage, these two men I chose as partners both needed to exercise dominance now and then through rituals of power. One of them was physically violent on a few occasions, a fact he always felt did not matter, and emotionally unkind quite consistently. My second longtime partner I chose in part because he was a major advocate for stopping violence against women, but as our bond progressed he began to be emotionally abusive now and then. It was as though he felt that I was too powerful, and that perception empowered him to challenge that power, to wound and hurt. I was stunned that the past was being reenacted in the present.

In self-help books galore the notion that women choose men who will treat them badly again and again is presented as truth. These books rarely talk about patriarchy or male domination. They rarely acknowledge that relationships are not static, that people change through time, that they adjust to circumstances. Men who may have seeds of negativity and domination within them along with positive traits may find the negative burgeoning at times of crisis in their lives.

The two men I chose as partners, like all the men I have loved, were victims of various degrees of emotional neglect and abandonment in their childhoods. They did not love their fathers or truly know them intimately. Growing from young adulthood into manhood they simply passively accepted the lack of communication with their fathers. They both felt that all attempts at reconciliation should have come from the father to the son. And yet as they matured into manhood, both these men began to behave not unlike the fathers whose actions they had condemned and hated. Observing them through time, I found that both of them had been rebellious and antipatriarchal in their twenties and early thirties, but as they moved more into the work world, they began to assume more of the patriarchal manners that identify one as a powerful and successful man. Though they had not been living with their fathers when it came time to be "men," the early models of their lives were unconsciously reenacted. They could have protected themselves from this intimate repetition only by consciously working to be different, only by being disloyal to the dominator model.

No man who does not actively choose to work to change and challenge patriarchy escapes its impact. The most passive, kind, quiet man can come to violence if the seeds of patriarchal thinking have been embedded in his psyche. Much of the Dr. Jekyll and Mr. Hyde behavior women describe in men who are alternately caring, then abusive has its root in this fundamental allegiance to patriarchal thinking. Indoctrination into the mind-set begun in childhood includes a psychological initiation that requires boys to accept that their willingness to do violent acts makes them patriarchal men. A distinction can and must be made between the willingness to do violent acts and actually doing them. When researchers looking at date rape interviewed a range of college men and found that many of them saw nothing wrong with forcing a woman sexually, they were astounded. Their findings seemed to challenge the previously accepted notion that raping was aberrant male behavior. While it may be unlikely that any of the men in this study were or became rapists, it was evident that given what they conceived as the appropriate circumstance, they could see themselves being sexually violent. Unconsciously they engage in patriarchal thinking, which condones rape even though they may never enact it.

This is a patriarchal truism that most people in our society want to deny. Whenever women thinkers, especially advocates of feminism, speak about the widespread problem of male violence, folks are eager to stand up and make the point that most men are not violent. They refuse to acknowledge that masses of boys and men have been programmed from birth on to believe that at some point they must be violent, whether psychologically or physically, to prove that they are men. Terrence Real calls this early indoctrination into patriarchal thinking the "normal traumatization" of boys:

> When I first began looking at gender issues, I believed that violence was a by-product of boyhood socialization. But after listening more closely to men and their families, I have come to believe that violence *is* boyhood socialization. The way we "turn boys into men" is through injury: We sever them from their mothers, research tells us, far too early. We pull them away from their own expressiveness, from their feelings, from sensitivity to others. The very phrase "Be a man" means suck it up and keep going.

> Disconnection is not fallout from traditional masculinity. Disconnection *is* masculinity.

This indoctrination happens irrespective of whether a boy is raised in a two-parent household or in a single female-headed household.

The perpetuation of male violence through the teaching of a dominator model of relationships comes to boy children through both women and men. Patriarchy breeds maternal sadism in women who embrace its logic. A great many women stand by and bear witness to their sons' brutalization at the hands of fathers, boyfriends, brothers, and so on because they feel by doing so they show their allegiance to patriarchy. No wonder then that male rage is often most directed at women in intimate relationships. Such relationships clearly trigger for many males the anger and rage they felt in childhood when their mothers did not protect them or ruthlessly severed emotional bonds in the name of patriarchy.

Contrary to popular myths, single mothers are often the most brutal when it comes to coercing their sons to conform to patriarchal standards. The single mom who insists that her boy child "be a man" is not antipatriarchal; she is enforcing patriarchal will. Researching boyhood, Olga Silverstein observed: "In single-parent families, it's common to see boys who have become their mother's 'little man.' Often these boys are very bossy children who patronize their mothers, who in fact do uncanny imitations of a certain kind of husband, being alternately possessive, protective, and seductive." Whether in single-parent or two-parent households, boys who are allowed to assume the role of "mini patriarch" are often violent toward their mothers. They hit and kick when their wishes are not satisfied. Obviously, as small boys they do not have the strength to overpower their mothers, but it is clear that they see the use of violence to get their needs met as acceptable. And while mothers of boys who hit them may feel that hitting is wrong, they may simultaneously feel that it is their job to meet the needs of any male, especially one who is coercive.

Many teenage boys have violent contempt and rage for a patriarchal mom because they understand that in the world outside the home, sexism renders her powerless; he is pissed that she has power over him at home. He does not see her autocratic rule in the home as legitimate power. As a consequence, he may be enraged at his mom for using the tactics of psychological terrorism to whip him into shape and yet respond with admiration toward the male peer or authority figure who deploys similar tactics. In patriarchal culture boys learn early that the authority of the mother is limited, that her power comes solely from being a caretaker of patriarchy. When she colludes with adult male abuse of her son, she (or later a symbolic mother substitute) will be the target of his violence.

Years ago the television show *The Incredible Hulk* was the favorite of many boys. It featured a mild-mannered scientist who turned into an angry green monster whenever he felt intense emotions. A sociologist interviewing boys about their passion for this show asked them what they would do if they had the power of the Hulk. They replied that they would "smash their mommies." In her groundbreaking work *The Mermaid and the Minotaur* feminist theorist Dorothy Dinnerstein highlighted the extent to which boys respond to the autocratic power of mothers with rage. Like many feminist researchers today, she insisted that male engagement with parenting was needed to break this projection onto the mother as an all-powerful figure who must be rebelled against and in some cases destroyed.

Clearly, patriarchal mothers who have rage at grown men act out with sons. They may either force the son to enter into an inappropriate relationship in which he must provide for her the emotional connection grown men deny her or engage in emotional abuse in which the son is constantly belittled and shamed. These acts of patriarchal violence serve to reinforce in the mind of boy children that their violence toward females is appropriate. It simply feels like justifiable vengeance. Feminist idealization of motherhood made it extremely difficult to call attention to maternal sadism, to the violence women enact with children, especially with boys. And yet we know that whether it is a consequence of power dynamics in dominator culture or simply a reflection of rage, women are shockingly violent toward children. This fact should lead everyone to question any theory of gender differences that suggests that women are less violent than men.

In patriarchal culture women are as violent as men toward the groups that they have power over and can dominate freely; usually that group is children or weaker females. Like its male counterpart, much female violence toward children takes the form of emotional abuse, especially verbal abuse and shaming, hence it is difficult to document. Maternal sadism must be studied, however, if we are to understand the roots of adult male violence toward women. To some extent the reformist feminist thinkers who have focused on women as the more ethical, kinder, gentler sex have stood in the way of an in-depth study of maternal sadism, of the ways women in patriarchal society act out violently with boys.

In our household growing up it was clear that our mother believed wholeheartedly that it was the role of the man to be a disciplinarian, to be in charge. When our dad used excessive violence, she merely saw it as his right. Lots of women who believe that it is the right of men to dominate feel that they should not resist male violence toward themselves or their children. Not surpisingly, these women, my mother included, use all manner of violence to discipline children. Fearful of being the objects of a grown man's rage, they may desire their children to be perfectly behaved so as not to arouse Daddy's ire.

In conversations with men whose mothers were passive as their sons were victimized by fathers or other male parental caregivers, I found that the men were far more likely than other men to idealize their moms, seeing them as victims without choice. While they did not direct anger toward their mothers and were often unable to even consider that she could have acted to protect their rights, these men were themselves violent in their intimate relationships with women. Their behavior affirms Terrence Real's insight that "the choreography of patriarchy, this unholy fusion of love, loss, and violence, spares no one." Mothers who ally themselves with patriarchy cannot love their sons rightly, for there will always come a moment when patriarchy will ask them to sacrifice their sons. Usually this moment comes in adolescence, when many caring and affectionate mothers stop giving their sons emotional nurturance for fear it will emasculate them. Unable to cope with the loss of emotional connection, boys internalize the pain and mask it with indifference or rage.

Usually adult males who are unable to make emotional connections with the women they choose to be intimate with are frozen in time, unable to allow themselves to love for fear that the loved one will abandon them. If the first woman they passionately loved, the mother, was not true to her bond of love, then how can they trust that their partner will be true to love. Often in their adult relationships these men act out again and again to test their partner's love. While the rejected adolescent boy imagines that he can no longer receive his mother's love because he is not worthy, as a grown man he may act out in ways that are unworthy and yet demand of the woman in his life that she offer him unconditional love. This testing does not heal the wound of the past, it merely reenacts it, for ultimately the woman will become weary of being tested and end the relationship, thus reenacting the abandonment. This drama confirms for many men that they cannot put their trust in love. They decide that it is better to put their faith in being powerful, in being dominant. In *Man Enough* Frank Pittman says of men that "while most of us want to be loved, controllers are willing to forego love if that is what it takes to be the boss." Being the boss does not require any man to be emotionally healthy, able to give and receive love.

Ever since I started writing about love, I have defined it in a way that blends M. Scott Peck's notion of love as the will to nurture one's own and another's spiritual and emotional growth, with Eric Fromm's insight that love is action and not solely feeling. Working with men who wanted to know love, I have advised them to think of it as a combination of care, commitment, knowledge, responsibility, respect, and trust. Most of our relationships have one or two of these aspects. Patriarchal men are schooled in the art of being responsible and giving instrumental care. As a teenager, when I complained about Dad's emotional neglect and abuse and his sporadic violence to Mama, she was always quick to remind me that he worked hard and provided for his family, that he was home almost every night, and for that reason alone we should respect and honor him. The fact that men often mix being caring and being violent has made it hard for everyone in our culture to face the extent to which male violence stands in the way of males' giving and receiving love.

The first act of violence that patriarchy demands of males is not violence toward women. Instead patriarchy demands of all males that they engage in acts of psychic self-mutilation, that they kill off the emotional parts of themselves. If an individual is not successful in emotionally crippling himself, he can count on patriarchal men to enact rituals of power that will assault his self-esteem. Feminist movement offered to men and women the information needed to challenge this psychic slaughter, but that challenge never became a widespread aspect of the struggle for gender equality. Women demanded of men that they give more emotionally, but most men really could not understand what was being asked of them. Having cut away the parts of themselves that could feel a wide rage of emotional response, they were too disconnected. They simply could not give more emotionally or even grasp the problem without first reconnecting, reuniting the severed parts.

Describing a couple in family therapy, Real recalls the qualities the wife wanted from her husband: "Sensitivity to others, the capacity to identify and share his feelings, a willingness to put his needs aside in the service of the family." These are the same qualities, Real points out, that "most boys, even in these enlightened times, have had stamped out of them." He concludes: "In our culture, boys and men are not, nor have they ever been, raised to be intimate." Women seeking intimacy from men often find their expressions of longing belittled. Many men respond to females' wanting emotional connection with emotional withdrawal and, in worst case scenarios, with abuse.

Emotionally self-mutilated, disconnected, many men make overtures of emotional connection only to later undermine these with emotional abuse. They simply do not get that love and abuse cannot go together. And why should they get it, when television shows, movies, and so much else in popular culture gives the message that any time there is intense passion between a couple, violence can erupt? Teaching men to understand that women and children do not feel loved when they are being abused, is one of the primary goals of groups that work to end male violence. Kay Leigh Hagan's autobiographical essay "A Good Man Is Hard to Bash" begins with the story of her dating a man who she felt was abusive and was potentially capable of physical violence. She calls his best male friend for advice about how much abuse she should endure, saying, " 'If I'm serious about him, and if I want the relationship to work, to last, there will be ups and downs. I don't think I should run away when it gets hard. I should be willing to tolerate a little abuse if I really love him.' " The friend looks her directly in the eyes and tells her, " 'Kay, in a loving relationship, abuse in unacceptable. You should not have to tolerate any abuse to be loved.' "

With characteristic boldness and radical honesty Hagan shares that her "understanding of love and power changed forever in that moment." She had imagined that her lover's friend would take his side: "Instead, his reaction encouraged me to love myself, to take responsibility for my own well-being, and to reject violence even in its subtler forms." Hagan was lucky to receive this wisdom early in life. The fate of most women is dramatically different, especially females who worship at the throne of patriarchy. These women feel, as Hagan did initially, that to choose to be with a patriarchal man is automatically to sign up for some level of abuse, however relative. Every day women explain away male violence and cruelty by insisting on gender differences that normalize abuse. Heterosexual women who are single and want to be with men feel that they cannot escape being victimized at some point by emotional and/or physical abuse at the hands of male partners. Collective female acceptance of male violence in love relationships, even if the appearance of acceptance masks rage, fear, or outright terror, makes it difficult to challenge and change male violence.

When the seemingly mild-mannered professor I lived with moved from emotional abuse to physical violence, I felt I should be understanding, forgiving. Like me, he had been raised in a dysfunctional family. However, even though he went to therapy, even though his physical violence stopped, he never really believed that he had done anything wrong. He harbored the notion, as many men who act violently do, that I was responsible for his bad behavior. In Donald Dutton's work with men who are violent, he identifies women's seeing behind the male mask as a catalyst for male violence:

> He may apologize and feel shame immediately after, but he can't sustain that emotion; it's too painful, too reminiscent of hurts long buried. So he blames it on her. If it happens repeatedly with more than one woman, he goes from blaming her to blaming "them." His personal shortcomings become rationalized by an evolving misogyny. . . . At this point the abusiveness is hardwired into the system. The man is programmed for intimate violence.

Often men who have been emotionally neglected and abused as children by dominating mothers bond with assertive women, only to have their childhood feelings of being engulfed surface. While they could not "smash their mommy" and still receive her love, they find that they can engage in intimate violence with partners who respond to their acting out by trying harder to connect with them emotionally, hoping that the love offered in the present will heal the wounds of the past. If only one party in a relationship is working to create love, to create the space of emotional connection, the dominator model remains in place and the relationship just becomes a site for continuous power struggle.

Women who stay in long-term relationships with men who are emotionally abusive or violent usually end up closing the door to their hearts. They stop working to create love. Often they stay in these relationships because a basic cynicism, rooted in their experience, affirms that most men are emotionally withholding, so they do not believe that they can find a loving relationship with any man. When I wanted to leave my first longtime partner, who had been continuously emotionally abusive and occasionally physically abusive, it was other women (my mother, close friends, acquaintances) who cautioned me about ending the relationship, letting me know that the man I was with was better than most men, that I was lucky. Leaving him was a gesture of self-love and self-reliance that I have not regretted. Yet I found that the observations of the women who cautioned me about what most men were like were fairly accurate.

The man I had lived with in partnership for almost fifteen years exhibited a mixture of patriarchal masculinity and alternative masculinity. We met during the heyday of feminist movement, and he was willing to work at creating gender equality. As it is for many men today, it was much easier for him to accept equal pay for equal work, sharing housework, and reproductive rights than it was for him to accept the need for shared emotional development. It is more difficult for men to do the work of emotional development because this work requires individuals to be emotionally aware—to feel. Patriarchy rewards men for being out of touch with their feelings. Whether engaged in acts of violence against women and children or weaker men, or in the socially sanctioned violence of war, men are better able to fulfill the demands of patriarchy if they do not feel. Men of feeling often find themselves isolated from other men.

This fear of isolation often acts as the mechanism to prevent males from becoming more emotionally aware.

When large numbers of young men in this nation rebelled against patriarchy to oppose the war in Vietnam, many of them were concerned with justice, many of them did not want to kill, but a great many simply did not want to die. To oppose war and the imperalism that promotes war placed these young men at odds with imperialist white-supremacist capitalist patriarchy. They suffered by choosing to take a stand. They were ridiculed by other men, more often than not represented as traitors. In the past ten years mass media have produced a number of movies aimed at boys that glorify war *(Saving Private Ryan, Independence Day, Men in Black, Blackhawk Down, Pearl Harbor,* to name a few) that once again make it appear heroic to die alone, away from home, fighting for a cause you may or may not understand. These movies are part of patriarchal antifeminist backlash. They glorify the patriarchal masculinity that enlightened women and men critique. They serve as propaganda, recruiting the hearts and imaginations of boys. Like gangsta rap, they celebrate male violence on all fronts, including the domination of women.

Conservative mass media offer daily lessons in patriarchal pedagogy; they tell boys what they must do to be men. In those homes where enlightened fathers daily work to repudiate violence, television reaffirms its importance, making courting death glamorous and sexy. Poor and working-class male children and grown men often embody the worst strains of patriarchal masculinity, acting out violently because it is the easiest, cheapest way to declare one's "manhood." If you cannot prove that you are "much of a man" by becoming president, or becoming rich, or becoming a public leader, or becoming a boss, then violence is your ticket in to the patriarchal manhood contest, and your ability to do violence levels the playing field. On that field, the field of violence, any man can win.

Men who win on patriarchal terms end up losing in terms of their substantive quality of life. They choose patriarchal manhood over loving connection, first foregoing self-love and then the love they could give and receive that would connect them to others. Feminist researchers have long since exposed the widespread domestic violence in our society. Yet since that exposure, violence against women has not declined and in some cases it has intensified. Antifeminist pundits seek to blame the intensification of male violence on women's greater equality. Yet most studies of family life indicate that in that sphere gender relations did not undergo any major revolution. Sociologist Arlie Hochschild has provided important data showing that domestic gender dynamics between men and women remain fairly sexist; women work outside the home but continue to do the lion's share of work in the home. Of course men who were covert misogynists before feminist movement felt more entitled to unleash their rage overtly as the movement gained momentum, but the rage was already present.

Male violence in general has intensified not because feminist gains offer women greater freedom but rather because men who endorse patriarchy discovered along the way that the patriarchal promise of power and dominion is not easy to fulfill, and in those rare cases where it is fulfilled, men find themselves emotionally bereft. The patriarchal manhood that was supposed to satisfy does not. And by the time this awareness emerges, most patriarchal men are isolated and alienated; they cannot go back and reclaim a past happiness or joy, nor can they go forward. To go forward they would need to repudiate the patriarchal thinking that their identity has been based on. Rage is the easy way back to a realm of feeling. It can serve as the perfect cover, masking feelings of fear and failure.

My father and mother have been married now for more than fifty years. Dad has never relinquished his patriarchal status and she has never challenged it. Yet by clinging to patriarchal thinking, they forfeited their chance to be happy together. The threat of violence, of emotional abuse, is always there, standing in the way of intimacy, keeping them from forgiving one another and starting over. Sadly, they are stuck in the trap of patriarchy. And it remains the breeding ground for everyday violence, the subtle, intimate terrorism that intensifies resentment and closes off the possibility of knowing joy.

It is not easy for males, young or old, to reject the codes of patriarchal masculinity. Men who choose against violence are simultaneously choosing against patriarchy, whether they can articulate that choice or not. In his insightful essay "Gender Politics of Men," R. W. Connell calls attention to the fact that men who oppose patriarchy remain at odds with the world they are living in:

> Men who try to develop a politics in support of feminism, whether gay or straight, are not in for an easy ride. They are likely to be met with derision from many other men, and from some

> women. It is almost a journalistic cliché that women despise Sensitive New Age Guys. They will not necessarily get warm support from feminist women.

Ultimately the men who choose against violence, against death, do so because they want to live fully and well, because they want to know love. These are men who are true heroes, the men whose lives we need to know about, honor, and remember.

5

Male Sexual Being

Most men and women are not having satisfying and fulfilling sex. We have all heard the notion that men come to relationships looking for sex and not love and that women come to relationships looking for love and not sex. In actuality, men come to sex hoping that it will provide them with all the emotional satisfaction that would come from love. Most men think that sex will provide them with a sense of being alive, connected, that sex will offer closeness, intimacy, pleasure. And more often than not sex simply does not deliver the goods. This fact does not lead men to cease obsessing about sex; it intensifies their lust and their longing.

If women have been taught through sexist socialization that a journey through the difficult terrain of sex will lead us to our heart's desire, men have been taught that their heart's desire should be for sex and more sex. Coming in the wake of sexual liberation, women's liberation seemed to promise heterosexual and bisexual men that women would begin to think the same way males do about sexuality, that female sexuality would become just as predatory, just as obsessive as male sexual desire. Lots of men thought this was the promise of paradise. Finally they were going to be able to go for the sexual gusto without having to worry about commitment. Sexist logic had convinced them and convinces them still that they can have connection and intimacy without commitment, that "Have dick will travel" meant that their needs could and would be met on command, at any time, anywhere.

In our culture these attitudes toward sexuality have been embraced by most men and many post-sexual liberation, postfeminist women. They are at the root of our cultural obsession with sex. When I first began to write books on love, to talk to lone individuals and then large audiences about the subject, I realized that it was practically impossible to have a serious discussion about love—that discussions of love, especially public conversations, are taboo in our society. Yet everyone talks about sex. We see all manner of sexual scenes on our television and movie screens. Talking about sex is acceptable. Talk shows engage audiences daily with explicit discussions of sexuality. Discussions of sex are fundamentally easier to engage in because in patriarchal culture sex has been presented to us as a "natural" desire. Most folks believe we are hardwired biologically to long for sex but they do not believe we are hardwired to long for love. Almost everyone believes that we can have sex without love; most folks do not believe that a couple can have love in a relationship if there is no sex.

Feminist movement was able to challenge and change notions of female inequality on many fronts, particularly in such arenas as work, education, and religion. However, sexism continues to shape the ways most people think about sexual relations. No matter how many men in our nation are celibate or have only occasional sexual experiences, people still believe that sex is something men have to have. Underlying this assumption is the belief that if men are not sexually active, they will act out or go crazy. This is why male-on-male sexual violence is accepted in our nation's prisons. This is why rape—whether date rape, marital rape, or stranger rape—is still not deemed a serious crime. This is why the rape of children, especially when conducted by mild-mannered, nice men, is allowed. If this were not so, celebrities accused of sexually abusing children would no longer be cultural icons. The assumption that "he's gotta have it" underlies much of our culture's acceptance of male sexual violence. It is why many people continue to believe that anyone who is raped may have "asked for it" by "seductive" dress or behavior, no matter how many television programs have aired the facts about sexual violence.

Children today learn more about sex from mass media than from any other source. Whether watching daytime soap operas, a porn channel, or X-rated movies, children in our nation are more aware of the body and of sexuality than ever before. Yet much of what they are learning about sexuality conforms to outmoded patriarchal scripts about the sexual nature of men and women, of masculine and feminine. They learn that in the world of sexual relations there is always a dominant party and a submissive party. They learn that males should dominate females, that strong men should dominate weaker men. They learn that whether he is homosexual or heterosexual, a man deprived of sexual access will ultimately be sexual with any body. If deprived long enough, even if he is straight he will have sex with another man; if he's gay, deprivation will lead him to engage in desperate sexual acts with women. Again and again children hear the message from mass media that when it comes to sex, "he's gotta have it." Adults may know better, from their own experience, but children become true believers. They think that men will go mad if they cannot act sexually. This is the logic that produces what feminist thinkers call "a rape culture."

Males, whether gay or straight, learn early on in life that one of the primary rewards offered to them for obedience to patriarchal thought and practice is the right to dominate females sexually. And if no female is around, they have the right to place a weaker male in the "female" position. In the anthology *Victims No Longer: Men Recovering from Incest and Other Sexual Child Abuse,* men who have been victimized by stronger boys, brothers, and other male peers share how the logic of patriarchal thinking about the right of the strong to do as they wish with those whom they deem weak was presented to them by their abusers. This same logic has usually shaped the thinking about sexuality embraced by adult abusers. Ed writes of his older brother's sexual abuse of him: "I learned about sex when I was nine years old. I was giving blow jobs at ten. While other kids were out playing with guns, I was learning how to 'please' a man. I was taught how to be a 'woman.' My brother liked to act out fantasies in which he was the 'man' and I was the 'woman.' " This older brother married and took with him into marriage the notion that it was his right to have sex with anyone he desired, whether they wanted to or not. His need to dominate was the salient feature in all his sexual relationships.

Within a culture of domination struggles for power are enacted daily in human relationships, often assuming their worst forms in situations of intimacy. The patriarchal man who would never respond to demands from his boss with overt rage and abuse will respond with fury when intimates want him to change his behavior. Men who do not daily lie and cheat at their jobs do so in their intimate bonds. This lying is usually connected to inappropriate sexual behavior or to discomfort about sexual behavior. In his powerful essay "Who He Was," Eric Guitierrez recounts how he told lies to cover up the reality that his father was gay: "About the same time I began lying about my father I began lying about myself. I didn't offer my lies indiscriminately. . . . Rather than making up comforting details that would portray my flashing, gay father more like the hardworking, lawn-mowing dads that lined our street, I instead embellished his shortcomings, his weaknesses, his rages, into real perversity. . . . I enthralled my classmates with stories of how my father would tie us up or throw crystal goblets at my terrorized mother. . . . I was an accomplished liar, building false identities for my father and myself by overstating truth on its own trajectory." Lying about sexuality is an accepted part of patriarchal masculinity. Sex is where many men act out because it is the only social arena where the patriarchal promise of dominion can be easily realized. Without these perks, masses of men might have rebelled against patriarchy long ago.

Little boys learn early in life that sexuality is the ultimate proving ground where their patriarchal masculinity will be tested. They learn early that sexual desire should not be freely expressed and that females will try to control male sexuality. For boys this issue of control begins with the mother's response to his penis; usually she does not like it and she does not know what to do with it. Her discomfort with his penis communicates that there is something inherently wrong with it. She does not communicate to the boy child that his penis is wonderful, special, marvelous. This same fear of the boy's penis is commonly expressed by fathers who simply do not concern themselves with educating boys about their bodies. Sadly, unenlightened approaches to child abuse lead many parents to fear celebration of their child's body, especially the boy body, which may respond to playful physical closeness with an erection. In patriarchal culture everyone is encouraged to see the penis, even the penis of a small boy, as a potential weapon. This is the psychology of a rape culture. Boys learn that they should identify with the penis and the potential pleasure erections will bring, while simultaneously learning to fear the penis as though it were a weapon that could backfire, rendering them powerless, destroying them. Hence the underlying message boys receive about sexual acts is that they will be destroyed if they are not in control, exercising power.

Adolescent sexual socialization is the vulnerable moment in a boy's life when he is required to identify his selfhood and his sexuality with patriarchal masculinity; it is the meeting place of theory and practice. During these formative years, when a boy's sexual lust is often intense, he learns that patriarchal culture expects him to covertly cultivate that lust and the will to satisfy it while engaging in overt acts of sexual repression. This splitting is part of the initiation into patriarchal masculinity; it is a rite of passage. The boy learns as well that females are the enemy when it comes to the satisfaction of sexual desire. They are the group that will impose on the boy the need to repress his sexual longings, and yet to prove his manhood, he must dare to move past repression and engage in sexual acts.

Sexual repression fuels the lust of boys and men. Shedding light on the negative impact of this socialization in the essay "Fuel for Fantasy: The Ideological Construction of Male Lust," Michael S. Kimmel demonstrates that sexual repression creates the world in which males must engage constantly in sexual fantasy, eroticizing the nonsexual. Exploring the link between sexual repression and sexism, he explains:

> Sexual pleasure is rarely the goal in a sexual encounter, something far more important than mere pleasure is on the line, our sense of ourselves as men. Men's sense of sexual scarcity and an almost compulsive need for sex to confirm manhood feed each other, creating a self-perpetuating cycle of sexual deprivation and despair. And it makes men furious at women for doing what women are taught to do in our society: saying no.

Despair and rage are the feelings men bring to sex, whether with women or with other men.

Encouraged to relate to sex in an addictive way by the patriarchal thinking which says "he's gotta have it," males must then adjust to a world where they can rarely get it, or never get it as much as they want, or where they can get it only by coercing and manipulating someone who does not want it, usually someone female. In *The Heart of the Soul* Gary Zukav and Linda Francis describe the characteristics of individuals addicted to sexual obsessions: "They cannot rest from thoughts of sex. They move from one encounter to the next. Each sexual experience brings only temporary relief from their craving, and it quickly returns. No amount of sexual activity can satisfy it." They explain that the "sexual craving is not for sex, but for something deeper." The fact that the craving always returns is the clue that addictive sexuality is not simply about getting sex. For the patriarchal male, be he straight or gay, addictive sexuality is fundamentally about the need to constantly affirm and reaffirm one's selfhood. If it is only through sex that he can experience selfhood, then sex has to be constantly foregrounded. Zukav and Francis explain: "The more intense the pain of fear, unworthiness, and feeling unlovable becomes, the more obsessive becomes the need to have a sexual interaction."

Sex, then, becomes for most men a way of self-solacing. It is not about connecting to someone else but rather about releasing their own pain. The addict is often an individual in acute pain. Patriarchal men have no outlet to express their pain, so they simply seek release. Zukav and Francis stress that the sex addict fears being inadequate and he fears rejection: "The stronger these emotions are, when there is no willingness to feel them, the stronger becomes the obsession with sex." Male sexual obsession tends to be seen as normal. Thus the culture as a whole colludes in requiring of men that they discount and disown their feelings, displacing them all onto sex. Steve Bearman makes this point in the essay "Why Men Are So Obsessed with Sex," explaining that "even if we do not engage compulsively in anonymous casual sex, pornography, masturbation, or fetishistic attempts to recover what has been forgotten, sex nevertheless takes on an addictive character." Whether straight or gay, male sexuality assumes this addictive character.

Since it is neither possible biologically nor practical, given the few hours in a day available for leisure activity, for men to be in sexual interactions constantly, patriarchal pornography available in myriad forms becomes the site of sublimation, the place where the sexual addict can get a quick fix. Patriarchal men can do pornography anywhere all day long. They can watch movies, look at magazines, look at real females with a pornographic gaze, undress them, fuck them, dominate them. Kimmel contends that male consumption of pornography is fed by the sexual lust males are taught to feel all the time and their rage that this lust cannot be satisfied:

> Pornography can sexualize that rage, and it can make sex look like revenge. . . . Everywhere, men are in power, controlling virtually all the economic, political, and social institutions of society. Yet individual men do not feel powerful—far from it. Most men feel powerless and are often angry at women, whom they perceive as having sexual power over them: the power to arouse them and to give or withhold sex. This

> fuels both sexual fantasies and the desire for revenge.

Many men are angry at women, but more profoundly, women are the targets for displaced male rage at the failure of patriarchy to make good on its promise of fulfillment, especially endless sexual fulfillment.

Men may be too terrified to confront the facts of their lives and tell the truth that possessing the right to engage in rituals of domination and subordination is not all that patriarchy promised it would be. If, as Terrence Real says, patriarchy were a disease, it would be a disease of "disordered desire"; to cure this disease, then, we would all need to reconsider the way we see men and male desire. Rather than seeing the violence men do as an expression of power, we would need to call it by its true name—pathology. Patriarchal violence is a mental illness. That this illness is given its most disordered expression in the sexual lives of men is powerful because it makes it hard to document since we do not witness what men do sexually like we witness what they do at work or in civic life. To take the inherent positive sexuality of males and turn it into violence is the patriarchal crime that is perpetuated against the male body, a crime that masses of men have yet to possess the strength to report. Men know what is happening. They simply have been taught not to speak the truth of their bodies, the truth of their sexualities.

Robert Jensen's powerful and courageous essay "Patriarchal Sex" drives this message home. Defining patriarchal sex, he writes: "Sex is fucking. In patriarchy, there is an imperative to fuck—in rape and in 'normal' sex, with strangers and girlfriends and wives and estranged wives and children. What matters in patriarchal sex is the male need to fuck. When that need presents itself, sex occurs." Boldly Jensen explains:

> Attention to the meaning of the central male slang term for sexual intercourse—"fuck"—is instructive. To fuck a woman is to have sex with her. To fuck someone in another context . . . means to hurt or cheat a person. And when hurled as a simple insult ("fuck you") the intent is denigration and the remark is often a prelude to violence or the threat of violence. Sex in patriarchy is fucking. That we live in a world in which people continue to use the same word for sex and violence, and then resist the notion that sex is routinely violent and claim to be outraged when sex becomes overtly violent, is testament to the power of patriarchy.

One might add that it is a supreme testament to patriarchy's power that it can convince men and women to pretend that sexual violence satisfies.

Much popular music from rock to rap shares this message. Whether it's Iggy Pop's lyrics, "I got my cock in my pocket and it's shoving up through my pants. I just wanna fuck, this ain't no romance" or the rap group Mystikals' lyrics, "When it's finished, over and done with it, I'm gonna smash a blount and knock the pussy off some bitch." Of course the truth of men's lives is that patriarchal sexuality has not satisfied. It has fueled the compulsive need to be more sexual, to be more violent in the hopes that there is a way to be more satisfied. Patriarchal pornography, no longer isolated but ever-present in popular mass media, has become so widespread because males brainwashed by the patriarchal mind-set cannot find the courage to tell the truth. They cannot find the courage to say, "I can't get no satisfaction." Patriarchal pornography has become an inescapable part of everyday life because the need to create a pretend culture where male sexual desire is endlessly satisfied keeps males from exposing the patriarchal lie and seeking healthy sexual identities.

Gay subcultures have historically articulated with greater honesty and boldness male compulsive sexual desire. And contrary to popular imagination, rather than being antipatriarchal, homosexual predatory sex is the ultimate embodiment of the patriarchal ideal. Jensen observes that "gay-or-straight doesn't much matter. The question of resistance to patriarchal sex is just as important in that gay men fuck in about the same way straight men do. We all received pretty much the same training. . . . Fucking is taken to be the thing that gay men do; some might even argue that if you aren't fucking, you aren't gay." More often than not, gay males, unless they have consciously decided otherwise, are as patriarchal in their thinking about masculinity, about sexuality, as their heterosexual counterparts. Their investment in patriarchy is an intensely disordered desire, because they are enamored of the very ideology that fosters and promotes homophobia. Now that patriarchal straight men have been compelled through mass media to face the fact that homosexual males are not "chicks with dicks," that they can and do embody patriarchal masculinity, straight male sexual dominance of biological females has intensified, for it is really the only factor that distinguishes straight from gay. Concurrently, homophobia becomes amplified among heterosexual men because its overt expression is useful as a way to identify, among apparently similar macho men, who is gay and who is straight.

Patriarchal pornography is a space of shared masculinity for straight and gay men. The images gay men seek are male, but males positioned in the same way as the male and female bodies of straight pornography. Whether catering to gay or straight males, patriarchal pornography is fundamentally a reenactment of dominator culture in the realm of the sexual.

Male "need" of patriarchal pornography that eroticizes domination is no show of male power. While hatred of women can lead to acts of domination that hurt, wound, and destroy, there is no constructive power here. Tragically, if masses of men believe that their selfhood and their patriarchal sexuality are one and the same, they will never find the courage to create liberating, fulfilling sexuality. It is this reality that leads men of conscience in patriarchal society to fear sex with the same intensity that females often fear sex. As Jensen testifies:

> I am afraid of sex as sex is defined by the dominant culture, as practiced all around me, and projected onto magazine pages, billboards, and movie screens. I am afraid of sex because I am afraid of domination, cruelty, violence, and death. I am afraid of sex because sex has hurt me and hurt lots of people I know, and because I

> have hurt others with sex in the past. I know that there are people out there who have been hurt by sex in ways that are beyond words, who have experienced a depth of pain that I will never fully understand. And I know there are people who are dead because of sex. Yes, I am afraid of sex. How could I not be?

Despite the courageous testimony of Jensen and others, despite the radical critique of patriarchal sex, most men are not breaking through denial and telling the truth about sex. They are choking it down, the pain, the despair, the confusion: they are following the patriarchal rules.

Rather than change, patriarchal males and females have exploited the logic of gender equality in the sexual realm to encourage women to be advocates of patriarchal sex and to pretend, like their male counterparts, that this is sexual freedom. Music videos and televisions shows like *Sex and the City* (written and produced by patriarchal men and women) teach females, especially young females, that the desirable female companion is one who is willing to play either a dominant or a subordinate role, one who can be as nonchalant about sex as any patriarchal man. Socializing women to conform more to patriarchal male sexual norms is one way patriarchy hopes to address male rage. Since this rage covers up the pain that could be the catalyst for critical awakening, it has to be assuaged. It is not just antifeminist backlash that has led to the normalization of pornographic sexual violence in our mass media and in common sexual practice; the desire to keep men from feeling and naming their pain fuels the need for consistent brainwashing.

Male despair, often initially expressed as anger, is a far greater threat to the patriarchal sexual order than feminist movement. While masses of men continue to use patriarchal sex and pornography to numb themselves, many men are weary of numbing and are trying to find a way to reclaim selfhood. This process of recovery includes finding a new sexuality. The assault on the male body by modern diseases, lowered sex drive, and out-and-out impotence has caused individual men not only to question patriarchal sex but to the find new ways of being sexual that can satisfy.

If unenlightened men are suffering their version of the "problem that has no name" when it comes to sexuality, they can ease their pain by breaking through denial and repudiating the patriarchal script of domination and submission. With keen insight Bearman in the essay "Why Men Are So Obsessed with Sex" reminds males that they have a choice:

> Directly and indirectly, we are handed sexuality as the one vehicle through which it might still be possible to express and experience essential aspects of our humanness that have been slowly and systematically conditioned out of us. Sex was, and is, presented as the road to real intimacy, complete closeness, as the arena in which it is okay to openly love, to be tender and vulnerable and yet remain safe, to not feel so deeply alone. Sex is the one place sensuality seems to be permissible, where we can be gentle with our own bodies and allow ourselves our overflowing passion. This is why men are so obsessed with sex. . . .

> But in no way can sex completely fulfill these needs. Such needs can only be fulfilled by healing from the effects of male conditioning and suffusing every area of our lives with relatedness and aliveness.

Compulsive sexuality, like any addiction, is hard for men to change because it takes the place of the healing that is needed if men are to love their bodies and let that love lead them into greater community with other human bodies, with the bodies of women and children.

Bearman reminds men that "no matter how much sex you encounter, it will not be enough to fill your enormous need to love and be close and express your passion and delight in your senses and feel life forces coursing through your muscles and skin." If masses of men could recover this fundamental passion for their own bodies, that shift away from patriarchal sex might lead us toward a true sexual revolution. To recover the power and passion of male sexuality unsullied by patriarchal assault, males of all ages must be allowed to speak openly of their sexual longing. They must be able to be sexual beings in a space where patriarchal thinking can no longer make violation the only means of attaining sexual pleasure. This is a tough job. And until males learn how to do it, they will not be satisfied.

6

Work: What's Love Got to Do with It?

Before feminist movement boys were more likely to be taught, at home and at school, that they would find fulfillment in work. Today boys hear a slightly different message. They are told that money offers fulfillment and that work is a way to acquire money—but not the only way. Winning the lottery, finding a wealthy partner, or committing a crime for which you do not get caught are paths to fulfillment that are as acceptable as working. These attitudes about the nature of work in patriarchal society have changed as capitalism has changed the nature of work. Few men, either now or in the future, can expect a lifetime of full employment. Nowadays working men of all classes experience periods of unemployment. In order to keep the faith, patriarchal culture has had to offer men different criteria for judging their worth than work.

As a primary foundation of patriarchal self-esteem, work has not worked for masses of men for some time. Rather than throw out the whole outmoded patriarchal script so that the nature of work in our culture can be changed, men are offered addictions that make unsatisfying work more bearable. Patriarchal obsession with sex and the pornography it produces are promoted to soothe men subliminally while they perform jobs that are tedious, boring, and oftentimes dehumanizing, jobs where their health and well-being are at risk. Most male workers in our America, like their female counterparts, work in exploitative circumstances; the work they do and the way they are treated by superiors more often than not undermine self-esteem.

One of the antifeminist patriarchal sentiments that has gained ground in recent years is the notion that masses of men used to be content to slave away at meaningless labor to fulfill their role as providers and that it is feminist insistence on gender equality in the workforce that has created male discontent. Underlying this assumption is the notion that women coming into the workforce, no longer looking to their men to be sole providers for the family, have undermined the well-being of men in patriarchal culture. Yet many sociological studies of men at work done prior to feminist movement indicate that males were already expressing grave discontent and depression about the nature and meaning of work in their lives. This discontent does not receive the attention that male workers receive when they blame their unhappiness with the world of work on feminist movement.

In her massive journalistic treatise *Stiffed: The Betrayal of the American Man,* Susan Faludi documents the reality that some males, especially older men, felt that changes in the valuation and nature of work, as well as competition with women for jobs, robbed them of the pride in being providers, creating what she calls a "masculinity crisis."

> The outer layer of the masculinity crisis, men's loss of economic authority, was most evident in the recessionary winds of the early nineties, as the devastation of male unemployment grew ever fiercer. The role of family breadwinner was plainly being undermined by economic forces that spat many men back into a treacherous job market during corporate "consolidations" and downsizings. Even the many men who were never laid off were often gripped with the fear that they could be next—that their footholds as providers were frighteningly unsteady.

Masses of men in our culture may believe that their ability to provide for themselves and families is a measure of their manhood, yet they often do not actually use their resources to provide for others.

Feminist theorists, myself included, have for some time now called attention to the fact that the behavior of men who make money yet refuse to pay alimony or child support, or their peers who head households yet squander their paycheck on individual pleasures, challenges the patriarchal insistence that men are eager to be caretakers and providers. Barbara Ehrenreich's *The Hearts of Men* was one of the first books highlighting the reality that many men are not eager to be providers, that the very idea of the "playboy" was rooted in the longing to escape this role and to have another means of proving one's manhood. Male heads of households who give a meager portion of their wages for the needs of their family can still have the illusion that they are providers. Nowadays women's income can be the backup money that allows many patriarchal men to squander their paycheck on drugs, alcohol, gambling, or sexual adventures even as they lay claim to being the provider.

Today's male worker struggles to provide economically for himself. And if he is providing for self and family, his struggle is all the more rigorous and the fear of failure all the more intense. Men who make a lot of money in this society and who are not independently wealthy usually work long hours, spending much of their time away from the company of loved ones. This is one circumstance they share with men who do not make much money but who also work long hours. Work stands in the way of love for most men then because the long hours they work often drain their energies; there is little or no time left for emotional labor, for doing the work of love. The conflict between finding time for work and finding time for love and loved ones is rarely talked about in our nation. It is simply assumed in patriarchal culture that men should be willing to sacrifice meaningful emotional connections to get the job done. No one has really tried to examine what men feel about the loss of time with children, partners, loved ones, and the loss of time for self-development. The workers Susan Faludi highlights in *Stiffed* do not express concern about not having enough time for self-reflection and emotional connection with self and others.

There is very little research that documents the extent to which depression about the nature of work leads men to act violently in their domestic lives. Contemporary patriarchy has offered disappointed male workers a trade-off: the perks of manhood that a depressed economy takes away can be redeemed in the realm of the sexual through domination of women. When that world of sexuality is not fulfilling, males rage. In actuality women are weary of male domination in the sexual sphere particularly, and rather than making for greater "domestic bliss," men's turning to sex for the satisfaction that they do not receive at work intensifies strife. The movement of masses of women into the workforce has not undermined male workers economically; they still receive the lion's share of both jobs and wages. It has made women who work feel more entitled to resist domination than women who stay home dependent on a man's wages to survive.

Working-class and middle-income women I have spoken with talk about the extent to which working outside the home after years of staying home bolstered their self-esteem and provided them with a different perspective on relationships. These women often begin to place greater demands on male spouses and lovers for emotional engagement. Faced with these demands, working men often wish that the little woman would stay home so that he could wield absolute power, no matter the amount of his paycheck. In many cases when a woman's paycheck is more than that of her male partner, he acts out to restore his sense of dominance. He may simply confiscate her paycheck and use it as he desires, thus rendering her dependent. He may increase his demands for sexual favors, and if that does not work, he can simply withhold sex, thus making a working woman who desires sex feel her power undermined.

Most women who work long hours come home and work a second shift taking care of household chores. They feel, like their male counterparts, that there is no time to do emotional work, to share feelings and nurture others. Like their male counterparts, they may simply want to rest. Working women are far more likely than other women to be irritable; they are less open to graciously catering to someone else's needs than the rare woman who stays home all day, who may or may not caretake children. Domestic households certainly suffer when sexism decrees that all emotional care and love should come from women, in the face of the reality that working women, like their male counterparts, often come home too tired to deliver the emotional goods. Sexist men and women believe that the way to solve this dilemma is not to encourage men to share the work of emotional caretaking but rather to return to more sexist gender roles. They want more women, especially those with small children, to stay home.

Of course they do not critique the economy that makes it necessary for all adults to work outside the home; instead they pretend that feminism keeps women in the workforce. Most women work because they want to leave the house and because their families need the income to survive, not because they are feminists who believe that their working is a sign of liberation. When individual men stay home to do the work of homemaking and child rearing, the arrangement is still viewed as "unnatural" by most observers. Rather than being viewed as doing what they should do as people in relationships, homemaking men are seen as especially chivalrous, as sacrificing the power and privileges they could have as privileged male workers outside the home in order to do woman's work inside the home.

It has been through assuming the role of participatory

loving parents that individual men have dared to challenge sexist assumptions and do work in the home that also invites them to learn relational skills. They document the rightness of feminist theory that argues that if men participated equally in child rearing, they would, like their female counterparts, learn how to care for the needs of others, including emotional needs. Even though more men actively parent to some degree than ever before in our nation's history, the vast majority of men still refuse to play an equal role in the emotional development of their children. They often use work as the excuse for emotional estrangement. Whether they regard themselves as pro- or antifeminist, most women want men to do more of the emotional work in relationships. And most men, even those who wholeheartedly support gender equality in the workforce, still believe that emotional work is female labor. Most men continue to uphold the sexist decree that emotions have no place in the work world and that emotional labor at home should be done by females.

Many men use work as the place where they can flee from the self, from emotional awareness, where they can lose themselves and operate from a space of emotional numbness. Unemployment feels so emotionally threatening because it means that there would be time to fill, and most men in patriarchal culture do not want time on their hands. Victor Seidler expresses his fear of having downtime in *Rediscovering Masculinity,* confessing, "I have learned how hard it is to give myself time, even an hour for myself a day. There are always things I am supposed to be doing. A feeling of panic and anxiety emerges at the very thought of spending more time with myself." He argues that most men have such a limited sense of self that they are uncertain that they possess "selves we could want to relate to." He contends, "We only seem to learn that the 'self' is something we have to control tightly, since otherwise it might upset our plans. . . . We never really give ourselves much chance to know ourselves better or develop more contact with ourselves, since . . . all this threatens the 'control' we have been brought up to identify our masculinity with. We feel trapped, though we do not know how we are constantly remaking this trap for ourselves." Competition with other men in the workplace can make it all the more difficult for men to express feelings or to take time alone. The male who seeks solitude in the workplace, especially during down-times, is seen as suspect. Yet when men gather together at work, they rarely have meaningful conversations. They jeer, they grandstand, they joke, but they do not share feelings. They relate in a scripted, limited way, careful to remain within the emotional boundaries set by patriarchal thinking about masculinity. The rules of patriarchal manhood remind them that it is their duty as men to refuse relatedness.

Even though male workers like Kenneth Blanchard, author of the *One Minute Manager* and coauthor of *The Power of Ethical Management*, share the wisdom that relational skills should be cultivated by men to improve the nature of work and work relations, most work settings remain places where emotional engagement between workers, especially a boss and a subordinate, is deemed bad for business. Were more men in touch with their relational skills and their emotional life, they might choose work that would at least sometimes enhance their well-being.

Although women with class privilege such as Susan Faludi or Susan Bordo who write about men express surprise that most men do not see themselves as powerful, women who have been raised in poor and working-class homes have always been acutely aware of the emotional pain of the men in their lives and of their work dissatisfactions. Had Susan Faludi read the work of feminist women of color writing about the poor and working-class men whom we know most intimately, she would not have been "surprised" to find masses of men troubled and discontent. Women with class privilege have been the only group who have perpetuated the notion that men are all-powerful, because often the men in their families *were* powerful. When Faludi critiques the popular feminist notion that men are all-powerful, she counts on the ignorance of readers about feminist writing to perpetuate the notion that feminists have not understood male pain. It serves her argument to promote this inaccurate portrait.

Visionary feminists were writing about the fact that working-class men, far from feeling powerful, were terribly wounded by the patriarchy long before Faludi conceived of *Stiffed,* and it is difficult to imagine that she was not aware of that writing. It is disingenuous of her as well to act as though the liberation movement that women created to confront their "problem with no name" addressed women cross class lines. Feminist movement has had very little impact on the masses of working-class women who were in the workforce prior to the movement and who still remain there, just as dissatisfied and discontent with their lot as the men in their lives. Poor and working-class women have always known that the everyday work experience places men in an environment where they feel powerless and where they are unable to articulate that on patriarchal terms; to use Faludi's words, they feel "less than masculine."

Just as feminist gains in this nation primarily had a positive impact on women with class privilege, the "working" men who have been given permission within the contours of patriarchal culture to reconfigure the nature of work in their lives tend to have class power. In the late eighties and early nineties a number of popular movies portrayed powerful men either through illness or crisis evaluating their lives and choosing to make profound changes in the nature of work. In the recent film *Life as a House* a white male architect whose work is being devalued quits, finds out that he has cancer and only a short time to live, then engages in a process of rethinking patriarchy, though of course that term is not used. Evaluating his life, he chooses to use his remaining months to make emotional connections with family, especially his teenage son, and with friends. He spends his time learning how to give and receive love. His ex-wife's wealthy businessman husband, inspired by the example of the dying man, and rethinks the nature of his life and resolves to give less time to work and more time to emotional connections. This film, like its predecessors, makes clear that working men must make time to get in touch with their emotional selves if they are to become men of feeling.

The immensely popular Academy Award–winning movie *American Beauty* showed the primary character, Lester Burnham, depressed about his life, his work, his marriage, and his family; he has lost his capacity to feel. He stops taking work seriously and by the end is getting in touch with his feelings, yet he cannot redeem his life. He also dies, like the protagonist in *Life as a House.* These movies seduce audiences with images of men in the process of growing up, but then they betray their characters and us by never letting these men live. They echo the patriarchal message that if a man stops work, he loses his reason for living. In *Rediscovering Masculinity* Victor Seidler states that the male who defines his self through work seeks to do so because "this is the only identity that can traditionally belong to us . . . believing we can still prove our masculinity by showing we do not need anything from others." In *American Beauty* Lester suffers alone. His critical investigation of his feelings takes place in his head. And he cannot survive being so utterly vulnerable and isolated. Ultimately, movies send the message to male audiences that men will not be meaningfully empowered if they learn to love. *American Beauty* finally tells audiences that there is no hope for depressed men who are willing to critically reflect on their lives. It tells us that even when men are willing to change, there is no place for them in patriarchal culture. The opening lines of the film say it all: "My name is Lester Burnham. I am forty-two. In less than a year I'll be dead. Of course, I don't know that yet. And anyway, I'm dead already." Popular culture offers us few or no redemptive images of men who start out emotionally dead. Unlike Sleeping Beauty, they cannot be brought back to life. In actuality, individual men are engaged in the work of emotional recovery every day, but the work is not easy because they have no support systems within patriarchal culture, especially if they are poor and working-class. And it is no accident that

Life as a House, which shows a man rejecting patriarchy and finding his way, is not as successful as *American Beauty.*

Poor and working-class men suffering job depression, despair about the quality of their intimate lives, a feeling of alienation, or a sense of being lost often turn to substance abuse to ease their pain. When they begin to seek recovery, AA is one of the few places they can go to do the work of getting well. In healing groups they learn first and foremost that it is important to be in touch with their feelings, that they have a right to name those feelings. The success of AA is tied to the fact that the practice of recovery takes place in the context of community, one in which shame about failure can be expressed and male longing for healing validated. Visionary male healers, such as John Bradshaw, found the way to healing in these settings. Working-class men I have interviewed who found in recovery the way back to emotional connection share that it is profoundly difficult to engage in this work, which is fundamentally anti-patriarchal, and then leave these settings to reenter patriarchal culture. One man talked about how his female partner was turned off by his willingness to express feelings, to tell his story; in her eyes this was weakness. She insisted that now that he was sober he did not need to "express these feelings" anymore.

Despite changes in the nature of gender roles, ours is still a patriarchal culture where sexism rules the day. If it were not so men could see periods of unemployment as time-outs where they could do the work of self-actualization, where they could do the work of healing. Many working men in our culture can barely read or write. Imagine if time away from work could be spent in exciting literacy programs for poor and working-class men. Imagine a wage offered for this work of self-development. When patriarchy no longer rules the day, it will be possible for men to view themselves holistically, to see work as part of life, not their whole existence. In *Love and Survival* Dean Ornish, sharing his personal struggle to work less, to make time for self-actualization, offers this insight:

> If the intention behind the work is to seek recognition and power—"hey, look at me, I'm special, I'm important, I'm worthy of your love and respect"—then you are setting yourself apart from others as a way of trying to feel connected to them. Setting yourself apart from others as a way of trying to feel connected to them: It seems so clear why this is self-defeating, and yet it is often the norm in our culture. . . . When my self-worth was defined by what I did, then I had to take every important opportunity that came along, even if relationships suffered.

When he began to choose to live holistically, Ornish was able to change this thinking about work.

Gail Sheehy's *Understanding Men's Passages* contains autobiographical accounts by men wrestling with the knowledge that the work they do is promoting severe depression and unhappiness. These men grapple with choosing their emotional well-being over the paycheck, over the image of themselves as a provider. Lee May recalls, "I was faced with two hard choices. One, stay in the job I was doing and choke, strangle, die psychologically, or quit and face the possibility that we would crumble financially." He admits that his unhappiness with work had undermined the spirit of well-being in his home: "Our household was an unhappy place. But had I stayed at the old jobs, my unhappiness would have pervaded our relationship." May was able to make the choice to leave his unhappy job, and the work he went on to do—writing a book about his life as a globe-trotting journalist, writing a popular column on gardening—was all work that enhanced his self-awareness, his self-actualization. His honest portrayal of his fears in breaking through denial is a model for many men who would learn to honor their inner selves rightly in a world that tells them every day that their inner selves do not matter.

Courageously writing about how hard it was to break with the patriarchal values that had governed his thinking for years, Ornish shares that the practice of intimacy is healing: "I am learning that the key to our survival is love. When we love someone and feel loved by them, somehow along the way our suffering subsides, our deepest wounds begin healing, our hearts start to feel safe enough to be vulnerable and to open a little wider. We begin experiencing our own emotions and the feelings of those around us." Imagine a nonpatriarchal culture where counseling was available to all men to help them find the work that they are best suited to, that they can do with joy. Imagine work settings that offer time-outs where workers can take classes in relational recovery, where they might fellowship with other workers and build a community of solidarity that, at least if it could not change the arduous, depressing nature of labor itself, could make the workplace more bearable. Imagine a world where men who are unemployed for any reason could learn the way to self-actualization. Women workers find that leaving the isolation of the home and working in a communal setting enhances their emotional well-being, even when wages are low and in no way liberating (as some feminist thinkers naïvely suggested they might be). If men followed this example and used the workplace as a setting to practice relational skills, building community, the male crisis around work could be addressed more effectively.

Many men who have retired from jobs, particularly men over sixty in our culture, often feel that aging allows them to break free of the patriarchy. With time on their hands, they are often compelled by extreme loneliness, alienation, a crisis of meaning, or other circumstances, to develop emotional selves. They are the elders who can speak to younger generations of men, debunking the patriarchal myth of work; those voices need to be heard. They are the voices that tell younger men, "Don't wait until your life is near it's end to find your feeling, to follow your heart. Don't wait until it's too late." Work can and should be life-enhancing for all men. When daring men come to work loved and loving, the nature of work will be transformed and the workplace will no longer demand that the hearts of men be broken to get the job done.

7

Feminist Manhood

Say that you are feminist to most men, and automatically you are seen as the enemy. You risk being seen as a man-hating woman. Most young women fear that if they call themselves feminist, they will lose male favor, they will not be loved by men. Popular opinion about the impact of feminist movement on men's lives is that feminism hurt men. Conservative antifeminist women and men insist that feminism is destroying family life. They argue that working women leave households bereft of homemakers and children without a mother's care. Yet they consistently ignore the degree to which consumer capitalist culture, not feminism, pushed women into the workforce and keeps them there.

When feminist women told the world that patriarchy promotes woman-hating, the response was that feminists were being too extreme, exaggerating the problem. Yet when men who knew nothing about feminism claimed that feminists were man-hating, there was no response from the nonfeminist world saying that they were being too extreme. No feminists have murdered and raped men. Feminists have not been jailed day after day for their violence against men. No feminists have been accused of ongoing sexual abuse of girl children, including creating a world of child pornography featuring little girls. Yet these are some of the acts of men that led some feminist women to identify men as woman-hating.

Even though not all men are misogynists, feminist thinkers were accurate when we stated that patriarchy in its most basic, unmediated form promotes fear and hatred of females. A man who is unabashedly and unequivocally committed to patriarchal masculinity will both fear and hate all that the culture deems feminine and womanly. However, most men have not consciously chosen patriarchy as the ideology they want to govern their lives, their beliefs, and actions. Patriarchal culture is the system they were born within and socialized to accept, yet in all areas of their lives most men have rebelled in small ways against the patriarchy, have resisted absolute allegiance to patriarchal thinking and practice. Most men have clearly been willing to resist patriarchy when it interferes with individual desire, but they have not been willing to embrace feminism as a movement that would challenge, change, and ultimately end patriarchy.

Feminist movement was from the outset presented to most males via mass media as antimale. Truthfully, there was a serious antimale faction in contemporary feminist movement. And even though the man-hating women were a small minority of women's libbers, they received the most attention. Failing to care for women rightly, men through continual acts of domination had actually created the cultural context for feminist rebellion. In the chapter on "Feminist Masculinity" in my recent book *Feminism Is for Everybody,* I write: "Individual heterosexual women came to the movement from relationships where men were cruel, unkind, violent, unfaithful. Many of these men were radical thinkers who participated in movements for social justice, speaking out on behalf of the workers, the poor, speaking out on behalf of racial justice. However when it came to the issue of gender they were as sexist as their conservative cohorts. Individual women came from these relationships angry. They used that anger as a catalyst for women's liberation. As the movement progressed, as feminist thinking advanced, enlightened feminist activists saw that men were not the problem, that the problem was patriarchy, sexism, and male domination."

It was difficult for women committed to feminist change to face the reality that the problem did not lie just with men. Facing that reality required more complex theorizing; it required acknowledging the role women play in maintaining and perpetuating patriarchy and sexism. As more women moved away from destructive relationships with men, it was easier to see the whole picture. It was easier to see that even if individual men divested themselves of patriarchal privilege, the system of patriarchy, sexism, and male domination would still remain intact, and women would still be exploited and oppressed. Despite this change in feminist agendas, visionary feminist thinkers who had never been antimale did not and do not receive mass media attention. As a consequence the popular notion that feminists hate men continues to prevail.

The vast majority of feminist women I encounter do not hate men. They feel sorry for men because they see how patriarchy wounds them and yet men remain wedded to patriarchal culture. While visionary thinkers have called attention to the way patriarchy hurts men, there has never been an ongoing effort made to address male pain. To this day I hear individual feminist women express their concern for the plight of men within patriarchy, even as they share that they are unwilling to give their energy to help educate and change men. Feminist writer Minnie Bruce Pratt states the position clearly: "How are men going to change? The meeting between two people, where one opposes the other, is the point of change. But I don't want the personal contact. I don't want to do it. . . . When people talk about not giving men our energies, I agree with that. . . . They have to deliver themselves." These attitudes, coupled with the negative attitudes of most men toward feminist thinking, meant that there was never a collective, affirming call for boys and men to join feminist movement so that they would be liberated from patriarchy.

Reformist feminist women could not make this call because they were the group of women (mostly white women with class privilege) who had pushed the idea that all men were powerful in the first place. These were the women for whom feminist liberation was more about getting their piece of the power pie and less about freeing masses of women or less powerful men from sexist oppression. They were not mad at their powerful daddies and husbands who kept poor men exploited and oppressed; they were mad that they were not being giving equal access to power. Now that many of those women have gained power, and especially economic parity with the men of their class, they have pretty much lost interest in feminism.

As interest in feminist thinking and practice has waned, there has been even less focus on the plight of men than in the heyday of feminist movement. This lack of interest does not change the fact that only a feminist vision that embraces feminist masculinity, that loves boys and men and demands on their behalf every right that we desire for girls and women, can renew men in our society. Feminist thinking teaches us all, males especially, how to love justice and freedom in ways that foster and affirm life. Clearly we need new strategies, new theories, guides that will show us how to create a world where feminist masculinity thrives.

Sadly there is no body of recent feminist writing addressing men that is accessible, clear, and concise. There is little work done from a feminist standpoint concentrating on boyhood. No significant body of feminist writing addresses boys directly, letting them know how they can construct an identity that is not rooted in sexism. There is no body of feminist children's literature that can serve as an alternative to patriarchal perspectives, which abound in the world of children's books. The gender equality that many of us take for granted in our adult lives, particularly those of us who have class privilege and elite education, is simply not present in the world of children's books or in the world of public and private education. Teachers of children see gender equality mostly in terms of ensuring that girls get to have the same privileges and rights as boys within the existing social structure; they do not see it in terms of granting boys the same rights as girls—for instance, the right to choose not to engage in aggressive or violent play, the right to play with dolls, to play dress up, to wear costumes of either gender, the right to choose.

Just as it was misguided for reformist feminist thinkers

to see freedom as simply women having the right to be like powerful patriarchal men (feminist women with class privilege never suggested that they wanted their lot to be like that of poor and working-class men), so was it simplistic to imagine that the liberated man would simply become a woman in drag. Yet this was the model of freedom offered men by mainstream feminist thought. Men were expected to hold on to the ideas about strength and providing for others that were a part of patriarchal thought, while dropping their investment in domination and adding an investment in emotional growth. This vision of feminist masculinity was so fraught with contradictions, it was impossible to realize. No wonder then that men who cared, who were open to change, often just gave up, falling back on the patriarchal masculinity they found so problematic. The individual men who did take on the mantle of a feminist notion of male liberation did so only to find that few women respected this shift.

Once the "new man" that is the man changed by feminism was represented as a wimp, as overcooked broccoli dominated by powerful females who were secretly longing for his macho counterpart, masses of men lost interest. Reacting to this inversion of gender roles, men who were sympathetic chose to stop trying to play a role in female-led feminist movement and became involved with the men's movement. Positively, the men's movement emphasized the need for men to get in touch with their feelings, to talk with other men. Negatively, the men's movement continued to promote patriarchy by a tacit insistence that in order to be fully self-actualized, men needed to separate from women. The idea that men needed to separate from women to find their true selves just seemed like the old patriarchal message dressed up in a new package.

Describing the men's movement spearheaded by Robert Bly in her essay "Feminism and Masculinity," Christine A. James explains:

> Bly claims that women, primarily since feminism, have created a situation in which men, especially young men, feel weak, emasculated, and unsure of themselves, and that older men must lead the way back. . . . Bly holds up the myth of the Wild Man as an exemplar of the direction men must take and never challenges the hierarchical dualisms that are so integrally linked to the tension he perceives between men and women. Arguably, the notion of the Wild Man merely reinforces clichés about "real masculinity" instead of trying to foster a new relationship between men and women, as well as the masculine and feminine.

The men's movement was often critical of women and feminism while making no sustained critique of patriarchy. Ultimately it did not consistently demand that men challenge patriarchy or envision liberating models of masculinity.

Many of the New Age models created by men reconfigure old sexist paradigms while making it seem as though they are offering a different script for gender relations. Often the men's movement resisted macho patriarchal models while upholding a vision of a benevolent patriarchy, one in which the father is the ruler who rules with tenderness and kindness, but he is still in control. In the wake of feminist movement and the diverse men's liberation movements that did not bring women and men closer together, the question of what the alternative to patriarchal masculinity might be must still be answered.

Clearly, men need new models for self-assertion that do not require the construction of an enemy "other," be it a woman or the symbolic feminine, for them to define themselves against. Starting in early childhood, males need models of men with integrity, that is, men who are whole, who are not divided against themselves. While individual women acting as single mothers have shown that they can raise healthy, loving boys who become responsible, loving men, in every case where this model of parenting has been successful, women have chosen adult males—fathers, grandfathers, uncles, friends, and comrades—to exemplify for their sons the adult manhood they should strive to achieve.

Undoubtedly, one of the first revolutionary acts of visionary feminism must be to restore maleness and masculinity as an ethical biological category divorced from the dominator model. This is why the term patriarchal masculinity is so important, for it identifies male difference as being always and only about the superior rights of males to dominate, be their subordinates females or any group deemed weaker, by any means necessary. Rejecting this model for a feminist masculinity means that we must define maleness as a state of being rather than as performance. Male being, maleness, masculinity must stand for the essential core goodness of the self, of the human body that has a penis. Many of the critics who have written about masculinity suggest that we need to do away with the term, that we need "an end to manhood." Yet such a stance furthers the notion that there is something inherently evil, bad, or unworthy about maleness.

It is a stance that seems to be more a reaction to patriarchal masculinity than a creative loving response that can separate maleness and manhood from all the identifying traits patriarchy has imposed on the self that has a penis. Our work of love should be to reclaim masculinity and not allow it to be held hostage to patriarchal domination. There is a creative, life-sustaining, life-enhancing place for the masculine in a nondominator culture. And those of us committed to ending patriarchy can touch the hearts of real men where they live, not by demanding that they give up manhood or maleness, but by asking that they allow its meaning to be transformed, that they become disloyal to patriarchal masculinity in order to find a place for the masculine that does not make it synonymous with domination or the will to do violence.

Patriarchal culture continues to control the hearts of men precisely because it socializes males to believe that without their role as patriarchs they will have no reason for being. Dominator culture teaches all of us that the core of our identity is defined by the will to dominate and control others. We are taught that this will to dominate is more biologically hardwired in males than in females. In actuality, dominator culture teaches us that we are all natural-born killers but that males are more able to realize the predator role. In the dominator model the pursuit of external power, the ability to manipulate and control others, is what matters most. When culture is based on a dominator model, not only will it be violent but it will frame all relationships as power struggles.

No matter how many modern-day seers assure us that power struggles are not an effective model for human relations, imperialist white-supremacist capitalist patriarchal culture continues to insist that domination must be the organizing principle of today's civilization. In *The Heart of the Soul* Gary Zukav and Linda Francis make it clear that while humans may have needed to create external power to keep the species alive at one time, this is no longer the case: "With or without reverence, the pursuit of external power leads only to violence and destruction. It is an evolutionary modality that no longer works. It is the wrong medicine, and nothing can make it the right medicine again." Patriarchal masculinity teaches men that their selfhood has meaning only in relation to the pursuit of external power; such masculinity is a subtext of the dominator model.

Before the realities of men can be transformed, the dominator model has to be eliminated as the underlying ideology on which we base our culture. We already see that within patriarchal culture men can be more emotional, they can parent, they can break with sexist roles, but as long as the underlying principles are in place, men can never be truly free. At any moment this underlying patriarchal ethos can overshadow behaviors that run counter to it. We have already seen that many men changed their thinking for a time when feminist movement was a powerful force for social change, but then when the patriarchal thinking that undergirds our society did not change, as the energy of the movement began to wane, the old order began to reestablish itself. Sexist thought and action that had been harshly critiqued during the height of feminist movement have once again become more acceptable. Clearly, ending patriarchy is necessary for men to have collective liberation. It is the only resolution to the masculinity crisis that most men are experiencing.

To offer men a different way of being, we must first replace the dominator model with a partnership model that sees interbeing and interdependency as the organic relationship of all living beings. In the partnership model selfhood, whether one is female or male, is always at the core of one's identity. Patriarchal masculinity teaches males to be pathologically narcissistic, infantile, and psychologically dependent for self-definition on the privileges (however relative) that they receive from having been born male. Hence many males feel that their very existence is threatened if these privileges are taken away. In a partnership model male identity, like its female counterpart, would be centered around the notion of an essential goodness that is inherently relationally oriented. Rather than assuming that males are born with the will to aggress, the culture would assume that males are born with the inherent will to connect.

Feminist masculinity presupposes that it is enough for males to be to have value, that they do not have to "do," to "perform," to be affirmed and loved. Rather than defining strength as "power over," feminist masculinity defines strength as one's capacity to be responsible for self and others. This strength is a trait males and females need to possess. In *The Courage to Raise Good Men,* Olga Silverstein stresses the need to redefine male sex roles in ways that break with sexist norms. Currently, sexist definitions of male roles insist on defining maleness in relationship to winning, one-upmanship, domination: "Until we are willing to question many of the specifics of the male sex role, including most of the seven norms and stereotypes that psychologist Robert Levant names in a listing of its chief constituents—'avoiding femininity, restrictive emotionality, seeking achievement and status, self-reliance, aggression, homophobia, and nonrelational attitudes toward sexuality'—we are going to deny men their full humanity. Feminist masculinity would have as its chief constituents integrity, self-love, emotional awareness, assertiveness, and relational skill, including the capacity to be empathic, autonomous, and connected." The core of feminist masculinity is a commitment to gender equality and mutuality as crucial to interbeing and partnership in the creating and sustaining of life. Such a commitment always privileges nonviolent action over violence, peace over war, life over death.

Olga Silverstein rightly says that "what the world needs now is a different kind of man"—she posits that we need a "good" man—but this binary category automatically invests in a dominator model of either-or. What the world needs now is liberated men who have the qualities Silverstein cites, men who are "empathic and strong, autonomous and connected, responsible to self, to family and friends, and to society, and capable of understanding how those responsibilities are, ultimately, inseparable." Men need feminist thinking. It is the theory that supports their spiritual evolution and their shift away from the patriarchal model. Patriarchy is destroying the well-being of men, taking their lives daily.

When Silverstein does workshops focusing on changing sexist gender roles, it is women who question her about whether a male with the qualities described above can survive. She responds to their fear by pointing out these truths:

> Men aren't surviving very well! We send them to war to kill and be killed. They're lying down in the middle of highways to prove their manhood in imitation of a scene in a recent movie about college football. They're dying of heart attacks in early middle age, killing themselves with liver and lung disease via the manly pursuits of drinking and smoking, committing suicide at roughly four times the rate of women, becoming victims of homicide (generally at the hands of other men) three times as often as women, and therefore living about eight years less than women.

And I would add that many men striving to prove patriarchal masculinity through acts of brutal and unnecessary violence are imprisoned for life. Clearly, lots of women survive leading happy, fulfilling lives because we do not embrace an identity which weds us to violence; men must have the same choice.

Women are not the only group who cannot imagine what the world would be like if males were raised with wholeness of being. There seems to be a fear that if men are raised to be people of integrity, people who can love, they will be unable to be forceful and act violently if needed.

A Masai wise man, when asked by Terrence Real to name

the traits of a good warrior, replied, "I refuse to tell you what makes a good morani [warrior]. But I will tell you what makes a great morani. When the moment calls for fierceness, a good morani is very ferocious. And when the moment calls for kindness, a good morani is utterly tender. Now, what makes a great morani is knowing which moment is which." We see that females who are raised with the traits any person of integrity embodies can act with tenderness, with assertiveness, and with aggression if and when aggression is needed.

Men who are able to be whole, undivided selves can practice the emotional discernment beautifully described by the Masai wise man precisely because they are able to relate and respond rather than simply react. Patriarchal masculinity confines men to various stages of reaction and overreaction. Feminist masculinity does not reproduce the notion that maleness has this reactionary, wild, uncontrolled component; instead it assures men and those of us who care about men that we need not fear male loss of control. The power of patriarchy has been to make maleness feared and to make men feel that it is better to be feared than to be loved. Whether they can confess this or not, men know that it just is not true.

This fear of maleness that they inspire estranges men from every female in their lives to greater or lesser degrees, and men feel the loss. Ultimately, one of the emotional costs of allegiance to patriarchy is to be seen as unworthy of trust. If women and girls in patriarchal culture are taught to see every male, including the males with whom we are intimate, as potential rapists and murderers, then we cannot offer them our trust, and without trust there is no love.

When I was a girl, my father was respected as the patriarchal provider and protector in our family. And he was feared. That ability to inspire fear was to him the sign of real manhood. Even though the knowledge that our dad could take care of his own was comforting, the moment he unleashed that will to do violence on us—his loved ones—we lost him. We were left with just our fears and the knowledge that there was no emotional connection great enough to soothe and transform our father's violence, to keep him connected.

How many men have lost this bond of love via acts of relational violence, acting out the notion embedded in patriarchal masculinity that in every male there is a predator, a hunter hungry and ready for the kill? Silverstein argues that men suffer by the patriarchal insistence that they enact rituals of alienation that lead to "estrangement from women." She states, "As anybody who works with the elderly will tell you, when octogenarians utter their dying words, it's 'Mama' the men call for, never 'Daddy.' These men may not even be calling out for an actual mother but for the symbolic mama who stands for nurturance, care, connectedness, whose loving presence lets us know we are not alone."

Patriarchal masculinity insists that real men must prove their manhood by idealizing aloneness and disconnection. Feminist masculinity tells men that they become more real through the act of connecting with others, through building community. There is no society in the world made up of one lone man. Even Thoreau in his solitary cabin wrote to his mother every day. When John Gray tells readers in *Men Are from Mars, Women Are from Venus* that men will go into their cave—that is, that men will disassociate and disconnect—he is accurately describing patriarchal masculinity. But he never suggests that men can be fulfilled living their lives in the cave. However, many men caught in patriarchy's embrace are living in a wilderness of spirit where they are utterly and always alone.

Feminism as a movement to end sexist domination and oppression offers us all the way out of patriarchal culture. The men who are awakening to this truth are generally younger men, who were born into a world where gender equality is more a norm. Unlike older generations of men, they do not have to be convinced that women are their equals. These are the young males who take women's studies classes, who are not afraid to identify themselves as advocates of feminism. They are the feminist sons of feminist mothers. Hence in his afterword to his mother's book *The Courage to Raise Good Men,* Michael Silverstein praises his mother's work: "The notion that men who have lost touch with their mothers have lost touch with parts of themselves is a powerful one—powerful enough to provoke change. I am proud that my mother has had the courage to open these issues for me and herself, and for other mothers and their sons." These men are the living example of the ways feminist masculinity liberates men.

Older generations of men who have shifted from sexist thinking to feminist masculinity were often moved by the women in their lives to make changes in thought and action, but for many it was the experience of assuming an equal parenting role that really transformed their consciousness and their behavior. I have had many conversations with men who in parenting daughters suddenly find themselves enraged by patriarchal biases that they had been unaware of or cared nothing about until the moment when they saw sexism begin to threaten their daughters' action and being. Feminist theorists argued from the onset of the movement that were men to participate in parenting in a primary way, they would be changed. They would develop the relational skills often seen as innate in women. Parenting remains a setting where men can practice love as they let go of a dominator model and engage mutually with women who parent with them the children they share. Male domination does not allow mutual intimacy to emerge; it keeps fathers from touching the hearts of their children.

As long as men dominate women, we cannot have love between us. That love and domination can coexist is one of the most powerful lies patriarchy tells us all. Most men and women continue to believe it, but in truth, love transforms domination. When men do the work of creating selves outside the patriarchal box, they create the emotional awareness needed for them to learn to love. Feminism makes it possible for women and men to know love.

Visionary feminism is a wise and loving politics. It is rooted in the love of male and female being, refusing to privilege one over the other. The soul of feminist politics is the commitment to ending patriarchal domination of women and men, girls and boys. Love cannot exist in any relationship that is based on domination and coercion. Males cannot love themselves in patriarchal culture if their very self-definition relies on submission to patriarchal rules. When men embrace feminist thinking and practice, which emphasizes the value of mutual growth and self-actualization in all relationships, their emotional well-being will be enhanced. A genuine feminist politics always brings us from bondage to freedom, from lovelessness to loving.

> "Mutual partnership is the foundation of love. Feminist thought and action create the conditions under which mutuality can be nurtured."

A true comrade and advocate of feminist politics, John Stoltenberg has consistently urged men to develop an ethical sensibility that would enable them to love justice more than manhood. In his essay "Healing from Manhood" he shares that "loving justice more than manhood, is not only a worthy pursuit, it is the future." As Stoltenberg explains, "Choosing loyalty to manhood over selfhood leads inevitably to injustice . . . loving justice more than manhood relocates personal identity in selfhood—relationally, reciprocally, realistically." He, like other male advocates of feminist thinking, knows firsthand that it is no easy task for men to rebel against patriarchal thinking and learn to love themselves and others. Feminist masculinity offers men a way to reconnect with selfhood, uncovering the essential goodness of maleness and allowing everyone, male and female, to find glory in loving manhood.

8

Popular Culture: Media Masculinity

Mass media do the work of continually indoctrinating boys and men, teaching them the rules of patriarchal thinking and practice. One of the primary reasons the feminist demand that we challenge and change patriarchy had so little impact on males was that the theory was primarily expressed in books. Most men were not buying or reading feminist books. During the peak moments of white female-led contemporary feminist movement, the late sixties and early seventies, male authors contributed books that took on the issues of destructive masculinity, critiquing patriarchy. Books such as *The Male Machine, Men's Liberation, The Liberated Man, The Limits of Masculinity, For Men against Sexism, Being a Man,* and *White Hero, Black Beast* challenged male passive acceptance of stereotyped sex roles.

These books and the discussions they generated had nowhere near the impact on male consciousness that feminist books focusing on womanhood were having on female consciousness. For the most part these white male writers did not strive to reconceptualize masculinity; instead they encouraged men to learn behavior patterns previously associated with females. They all agreed that economic changes coupled with changes in the status of women had produced a crisis in masculinity.

Within modern advanced capitalist society, masculine power was traditionally seen as synonymous with the ability of males to provide financially. However, as more and more women have gained access to the work sphere, the sphere of provision, this centrally defining attribute of patriarchal masculinity has lost significance. Gender equality in the workforce freed lots of men to speak their truth that they were not necessarily interested in the role of provider. Many men were happy with the idea that feminism was teaching women that they should pay their own way. Concurrently, as feminist movement and the so-called sexual revolution changed the notion that sexual action and initiation were exclusively the province of males, another signifier of patriarchal masculinity lost meaning. Gender-based changes in the workforce and in sexual politics meant that sex roles were modified for a vast majority of people, especially females, yet even so, patriarchal notions of masculinity remained intact, even when those notions did not have a reality base. Hence the crisis in masculinity. A traditional institutionalized patriarchal social order was being challenged and changed even as there were no major changes in sexist thinking.

Men experiencing this crisis could either cling for security and safety to the underlying assumptions of patriarchal ideology or they could ally themselves with feminist efforts and struggle to create new conceptions of masculinity, new possibilities for the social formation of male identity. The men who chose change, who dared to ally themselves with feminist movement, were often gay or bisexual or in heterosexual relationships with radical feminist women. Many women in these relationships found that the men in their lives lost interest in transforming masculinity after the initial feminist fervor subsided.

Mainstream mass media, particularly movies and television, reflected the contradictions even as they continued to reinforce patriarchal thinking and action. Most men chose not to change, and conservative mass media supported their staying in place. Men's continued allegiance to a notion of masculinity that could no longer be fully realized on the old terms led them to place greater emphasis on their ability to dominate and control by physical force and abusive psychological terrorism. Compelled to work in a public arena where men no longer asserted patriarchal control (job supervisors and higher-ranking bosses might be female), these men could fully enact rituals of patriarchal domination only in the private sphere. As a consequence, despite feminist changes in the area of work, incidences of male violence against women and children were escalating. Mass media, especially television talk shows, focused on male violence without linking that focus to ending patriarchy. Male domination of women simply became a new form of mass entertainment (hence the money-making spectacle of the O. J. Simpson trial). In social relationships with other men outside the sphere of work, men were more compelled than ever to enact rituals of domination. Among black males, black-on-black homicide fast became the leading cause of death for males between the ages of sixteen and forty-five.

In the world of television, shows directed at children never stopped their sexist myth making. One of the most popular children's shows with a subtext about masculinity was *The Incredible Hulk.* A favorite of boys from diverse class and racial backgrounds, this show was instrumental in teaching the notion that for a male, the exertion of physical force (brutal and monstrous) was a viable response to all situations of crisis. When a sociologist asked young male viewers what they would do if they had the power of the Hulk, they said that they would smash their mommies. The Hulk was the precursor for the Power Ranger toys that are still popular along with more recent video games which allow boys to engage in violent ritualized play.

The hero of *The Incredible Hulk,* like the many television and movie heroes that have come in his wake, is the perfect candidate for inclusion in Barbara Ehrenreich's book *The Hearts of Men: American Dreams and the Flight from Commitment.* He is a man always on the run, unable to develop lasting ties or intimacy. A scientist by training (the ultimate personification of rational man), when he experiences anger, he turns into a creature of color and commits violent acts. After committing violence, he changes back to his normal white-male rational self. He has no memory of his actions and therefore cannot assume responsibility for them. Since he is (like the hero of a popular adult drama, *The Fugitive)* unable to form sustained emotional bonds with friends or family, he cannot love. He thrives on disconnection and disassociation. Like the men of the Beat generation, like the more recent men of Generation X, he is the symbol of the ultimate patriarchal man—alone, on the road, forever drifting, driven by the beast within.

The Incredible Hulk linked sexism and racism. The cool, level-headed, rational white-male scientist turned into a colored beast whenever his passions were aroused. Tormented by the knowledge of this transformation, he searches for a cure, a way to disassociate himself from the beast within. Writing about the connection between racism and the construction of masculinity in *White Hero, Black Beast,* Paul Hoch contends, "There is indeed a close interaction between the predominant Western conception of manhood and that of racial (and species) domination. The notion, originally from myth and fable, is that the summit of masculinity—the 'white hero'—achieves his manhood, first and foremost, by winning victory over the 'dark beast' or over the barbarian beasts of other—in some sense, 'darker'—races, nations and social castes." Recent movies like *Men in Black, Independence Day,* and *The Matrix* rely on these racialized narratives of dark versus light to valorize patriarchal white masculinity in the realm of fantasy. In our actual lives the imperialist white-supremacist policies of our government lead to enactments of rituals of white-male violent domination of a darker universe, as in both the Gulf War and the most recent war against Iraq. By making it appear that the threatening masculinity—the rapist, the terrorist, the murderer—is really a dark other, white male patriarchs are able to deflect attention away from their own misogyny, from their violence against women and children.

The popularization of gangsta rap, spearheaded by white male executives in the music industry, gave a public voice to patriarchy and woman-hating. However, by promoting the voices of young black males (in the beginning many of whom were coming from the underclass), ruling-class white males could both exploit their clients' longing for the trappings of patriarchal masculinity (money, power, sex) and simultaneously make their antifeminist messages the lessons that young white males would learn. Just as the conservative white men who control our government use individual black males—for example, Colin Powell—to preach the gospel of war to the American public (affirming the idea that the darker other is the threat that the heroic white male must annihilate), mass media demonization of black males as the epitome of brutal patriarchal masculinity deflects attention away from the patriarchal masculinity of white men and its concomitant woman-hating.

One of the ways patriarchal white males used mass media to wage the war against feminism was to consistently portray the violent woman-hating man as aberrant and abnormal. A perfect example of the lengths to which patriarchal white men will go to deny their patriarchal violence is offered in the PBS documentary about the Hillside Strangler. Viewers are able to watch psychiatrists talk with a white male serial killer who murdered adult women and two girls. It is a tale told in parts, each part highly dramatic and suspenseful. Viewers learn that the accused is a handsome, all-American white boy (I use the word "boy" because the commentators refer again and again to his boyish qualities) with a lovely blond wife and a baby son. We are told that he does not have the appearance of a villain, a killer. We learn that he is hardworking, well liked, etc. All these qualities made detectives and police (all white and male) reluctant to arrest him. He seemed to them to be an "unlikely suspect." Even after his arrest, white-male mental health care professionals were brought on the case to at least provide documentation that if this all-American white male did indeed commit all these violent crimes against females, he did so because he was insane.

Finally a shrewd doctor uncovers that the accused has been pretending to be insane to escape punishment. It seems he studied psychology before he committed his crimes so that he would know how to appear crazy. When the doctor finally "unmasks" him, the Hillside Strangler states, "A woman is nothing to me. I can kill her in a minute." As the trial closes and the white male judge reads his final comments on the case, he tells viewers that the Hillside Strangler was a misogynist, a man who hated women. Yet the judge does not link this misogyny to patriarchy or sexism or male domination. Instead we are told that the man's mother whipped him to express her anger toward a violent, no-good gambler husband. In the final analysis a woman is blamed for this man's violence against women—another case of "She made me do it." Nothing is said of his rationally thought-out strategy of dissimulation or of the way he deceived many women and other people by pretending to be a nice guy, by impersonating the benevolent patriarch.

Since contemporary feminist movement, the genre of the mystery novel has exploited such feminist issues as domestic violence, rape, and incest to create male villains who are misogynists. Novels from *Jagged Edge* to the more recent *The Analysand* exploit feminist themes even as they uphold the need for patriarchal violence. In a real world where more than 90 percent of violent crimes are committed by men, it is not surprising that popular culture offers both negative and positive models of the masculine. Woman-hating dominator men are consistently depicted as loners, who may have been abused as children and who were not able to adjust in normal society. Ironically, these "bad" men share the same character traits as the "good" men who hunt them down and slaughter them. In both cases the men dissimulate (take on various appearances and disguises to manipulate others' perception of their identity), and they lack the ability to connect emotionally with others.

In contemporary films such as *Good Will Hunting* the sensitive man is shown to have a violent undercurrent. In the movie Will is the working-class young adult who has the opportunity to become a healthy male if he can confront his traumatic childhood and learn to feel again. He is a cinematic portrait of a man in patriarchal culture trying to reclaim connections. Terrence Real writes about the film:

> As Will Hunting shows us, a man cannot connect with others and remain cut off from his own heart. Intimacy generates too many raw feelings. Contending with them is requisite work for staying close. Yet the stoicism of disconnection, the strategy of avoiding one's feelings, is precisely the value in which boys are schooled. . . . Empathy to oneself and others lies in a realm that has remained devalued and unexplored—the domain of women. . . . Both the roots of Will's pain and also his entitlement to run from it, inflicting it instead, on those he most cares for, lie at the heart of patriarchy—the masculine code into which all boys are inducted.

This patriarchal code is passed own through generations. The award-winning film *Monster's Ball* depicts three generations of white men: the ruling patriarch, who is a victim of hard living, drinking, and smoking, his obedient patriarchal son, who works as a prison warden, and the third generation, the grandson, who is also following in the footsteps of his elders.

To realize the patriarchal masculine ideal, these white men must learn to disconnect from their feelings. The ruling patriarch addresses his son with verbal abuse, telling him that "Your mother wasn't shit." Shaming is the way he maintains control. Racist and misogynist, he is blindly followed by his son until that moment when the grandson, who is deemed weak because he is antiracist and able to feel, confronts his father. The boy asks why the father does not love him and then shoots himself in the mouth. His suicide brings an end to the patriarchal cycle and leads to the transformation of his dad, who seeks redemption among the black people he has previously hated. No other contemporary film exposes the evil of patriarchy as masterfully as *Monster's Ball.* The path to redemption requires the repudiation of white-male patriarchal rule. Yet as in many of the films that portray men resisting patriarchy, in the end the shift is merely a move from violent dominator patriarch to benevolent nice-guy patriarch.

Contemporary books and movies offer clear portraits of the evils of patriarchy without offering any direction for change. Ultimately they send the message that male survival demands holding on to some vestige of patriarchy. In *Monster's Ball* the male who is really different, who is humanistic, feeling, antiracist, and longing to move past patriarchal pornographic objectification to genuine intimacy is a victim. He kills himself. Watching this film, no male will be inspired to truly challenge the system. In another film, *Igby Goes Down,* the father, who is in touch with his feelings, is schizophrenic. When he shares feelings of being unable to bear the weight of patriarchal responsibility with his son, Igby cannot make an emotional connection. Driven by his hatred for his mother, Igby embraces the cruelty of the world around him and only escapes being violent by choosing to become a fugitive, a man on the run in search of a self he cannot find. The vast majority of contemporary films send the message that males cannot escape the beast within. They can pretend. They can dissimulate, but they can never break patriarchy's hold on their consciousness.

Until we can create a popular culture that affirms and celebrates masculinity without upholding patriarchy, we will never see a change in the way that masses of males think about the nature of their identity. In *Good Will Hunting,* when faced with the possibility of knowing love, Will must make a choice. He must let go of his feelings of worthlessness and shame engendered by his traumatic past; he must choose life over death. His choice to love, to live, is the break with the patriarchal model that liberates his spirit. As viewers we celebrate his new awareness of his essential goodness, his redemption. His recovery gives us hope.

Mass media are a powerful vehicle for teaching the art of the possible. Enlightened men must claim it as the space of their public voice and create a progressive popular culture that will teach men how to connect with others, how to communicate, how to love.

9

Healing Male Spirit

Men cannot speak their pain in patriarchal culture. Boys learn this in early childhood. As a girl, I was awed by a man in my church, a deacon, who would stand before the congregation and speak his love for the divine spirit. Often in the midst of his testimony he would begin to weep, sobbing tears into a big white handkerchief. The girls and boys who witnessed his tears were embarrassed for him, for in their eyes he was showing himself to be weak. When he wept, the men who stood beside him turned their eyes away. They were ashamed to see a man express intense feeling.

I remembered this beautiful man of feeling in the autobiography of my girlhood, *Bone Black:*

> To her child mind old men were the only men of feeling. They did not come at one smelling of alcohol and sweet cologne. They approached one like butterflies, moving light and beautiful, staying still for only a moment. . . . They were the brown-skinned men with serious faces who were the deacons of the church, the right-hand men of god. They were the men who wept when

> they felt his love, who wept when the preacher spoke of the good and faithful servant. They pulled wrinkled handkerchiefs out of their pockets and poured tears in them, as if they were pouring milk into a cup. She wanted to drink those tears that like milk could nourish her and help her grow.

To counter patriarchal representations of men as being without feeling, in both the books I write for adults and those I write for children, I have endeavored to create images of men that demonstrate their beauty and integrity of spirit.

Though we rarely use the word "patriarchy," everyone knows how sexist masculinity has assaulted the spirits of men. Though wrong-minded in his implied blaming of women for the emotional deadness males feel, poet Robert Bly called on men to find the Wild Man within in hopes that they would in a safe space let their hearts speak, that they would howl, and cry, and dance, and play, and find again the spirit within. Of course men who participated in workshops such as those Bly conducted, let loose for a while and then journeyed back to their patriarchal world, leaving the wild spirit behind. Any reader of Robert Bly's *Iron John* can hear the mother blame in his words. And Bly is right to demand that we all look at the role mothers play in deadening the spirits of boy children, but he fails to acknowledge that such mothers in their acts of maternal sadism are really doing the work of patriarchal caretaking, doing what they were taught a good mother should do.

It is highly ironic that we are now living in a time when we are told to question whether mothers can raise sons, when so many patriarchal men have been taught the beliefs and values of patriarchy by mothers, firsthand. Many mothers in patriarchal culture express their rage at adult men by directing anger at their sons. In *The Power of Partnership* Riane Eisler explains: "Some women direct their suppressed anger against men they feel are weak or vulnerable—their sons for example. The psychologist David Winter found that women living in countries or periods of extreme male dominance tend to be very controlling of their sons, who are the only males it is safe for them to vent against. Women in these circumstances are often subtly, or not so subtly, abusive of their sons." Many mothers in patriarchal culture silence the wild spirit in their sons, the spirit of wonder and playful tenderness, for fear their sons will be weak, will not be prepared to be macho men, real men, men other men will envy and look up to.

Much of the anger men direct at mothers is a response to the maternal failure to protect the spirit of the boy from patriarchal harm. In one of the family therapy sessions Terrence Real writes about in *How Can I Get Through to You?* a son describes that moment when patriarchal culture intrudes on the emotional bond with his mother, and her acquiescence. The son recalls, " 'She was telling me. Let me go, darling. Just let me go. We know that your father's a brute. We live together in a world of refined feeling he can never understand. But you see, darling, I am helpless, aren't I? What am I to do?' " Every day mothers are ruthlessly and brutally terminating their emotional connection with male children in order to turn them over to patriarchy, whether to an actual unfeeling father or to a symbolic father. Boys feel the pain. And they have no place to lay it down; they carry it within. They take it to the place where it is converted into rage.

Learning to dissimulate, men learn to cover up their rage, their sense of powerlessness. Yet when men learn to create a false self as a way to maintain male domination, they have no sound basis on which to build healthy self-esteem. To always wear a mask as a way of asserting masculine presence is to always live the lie, to be perpetually deprived of an authentic sense of identity and well-being. This falseness causes males to experience intense emotional pain. Rituals of domination help mediate the pain. They provide an illusory sense of self, an identity. Poet and farmer Wendell Berry in *The Unsettling of America: Culture and Agriculture* suggests that "if we removed the status and compensation from the destructive exploits we classify as 'manly,' men would be found to be suffering as much as women. They would be found to be suffering for the same reason: they are in exile from the communion of men and women, which is the deepest connection with the communion of all creatures." Many men in our society have no status, no privilege; they receive no freely given compensation, no perks with capitalist patriarchy. For these men domination of women and children may be the only opportunity to assert a patriarchal presence. These men suffer. Their anguish and despair has no limits or boundaries. They suffer in a society that does not want men to change, that does not want men to reconstruct masculinity so that the basis for the social formation of male identity is not rooted in an ethic of domination. Rather than acknowledge the intensity of their suffering, they dissimulate. They pretend. They act as though they have power and privilege when they feel powerless. Inability to acknowledge the depths of male pain makes it difficult for males to challenge and change patriarchal masculinity.

Broken emotional bonds with mothers and fathers, the traumas of emotional neglect and abandonment that so many males have experienced and been unable to name, have damaged and wounded the spirits of men. Many men are unable to speak their suffering. Like women, those who suffer the most cling to the very agents of their suffering, refusing to resist sexism or sexist oppression. Their refusal is rooted in the fear that their weakness will be exposed. They fear acknowledging the depths of their pain. As their pain intensifies, so does their need to do violence, to coercively dominate and abuse others. Barbara Deming explains: "I think the reason that men are so very violent is that they know, deep in themselves, that they're acting a lie, and so they're furious. You can't be happy living a lie, and so they're furious at being caught in the lie. But they don't know how to break out of it, so they just go further into it." For many men the moment of violent connection may be the only intimacy, the only attainable closeness, the only space where the agony is released. When feminist women insist that all men are powerful oppressors who victimize from the location of power, they obscure the reality that many victimize from the location of victimization. The violence they do to others is usually a mirroring of the violence enacted upon and within the self. Many radical feminists have been so enraged by male domination that they cannot acknowledge the possibility of male suffering or forgive. Failure to examine the victimization of men keeps us from understanding maleness, from uncovering the space of connection that might lead more men to seek feminist transformation. Urging women to overcome their fear of male anger, Barbara Deming writes that men are "in a rage because they are acting out a lie—which means that in some deep part of themselves they want to be delivered from it, are homesick for the truth." She explains that "their fury gives us reason to fear, but also gives us reason to hope."

It has been terribly difficult for advocates of feminism to create new ways of thinking about maleness, feminist paradigms for the reconstruction of masculinity. Despite the successes of feminist movement, the socialization of boys—the making of patriarchal masculine identity—has not been radically altered. Feminist writing, whether fiction or theory, rarely focuses on male change. I am always disturbed when male students request references to literature that will serve as a guide as they struggle to interrogate patriarchy and create progressive identities, because there is so little literature to offer them. By contrast, I can offer countless references to any female student who tells me she is trying to critically understand and change sexist female roles. There needs to be more feminist work that specifically addresses males. They need feminist blueprints for change.

In a course on feminist theory I asked students to comment on a book, film, television show, or any personal experience that offers them examples of reconstructed, feminist masculinity. In a class of more than forty students there were few positive responses. Several students talked about the old John Sayles movie *The Brother from Another Planet* and his most recent film, *Sunshine State*. I called attention to

Alice Walker's novel *The Color Purple.* Often when this novel is discussed, Celie's transformation from object to subject receives attention but no one talks about the fact that the novel also chronicles Mister's transformation, his movement away from patriarchal masculinity toward a caring, nurturing self who is able to participate in community.

In feminist fiction radically new roles for men emerge. As a fantasy, *The Color Purple* provides a utopian vision of the process by which men who embody a destructive sexist masculinity change. In *The Color Purple* Walker portrays the techniques of patriarchal domination used by males to maintain power in the domestic household, writing graphic accounts of abuse and terrorism, yet she also portrays the process by which the dominating male acquires a new consciousness and new habits of being. Her utopian vision of male transformation does not place the sole burden of change on men.

Celie also must change her attitudes toward men. She must not only affirm Albert's transformation, she must understand and forgive him. Her acceptance enables him to rejoin the community, to embrace a vision of mutual partnership. At the end of the novel Celie says of Albert:

> After all the evil he done I know you wonder why I don't hate him. I don't hate him for two reason. One, he love Shug. And two, Shug use to love him. Plus, look like he trying to make something out of himself. I don't mean just that he work and he clean up after himself and he appreciate some of the things God was playful enough to make. I mean when you talk to him now he

> really listen, and one time, out of nowhere in the conversation us was having, he said, Celie, I'm satisfied this the first time I ever lived on Earth as a natural man. It feel like a new experience.

To change, Albert must understand why he has abused women. He locates that will to abuse in the trauma of his upbringing when he is coerced to choose against his true self as part of being indoctrinated into patriarchy. Dehumanized himself, it is easy for him to feel justified in dehumanizing others. Near the end of the book, Albert becomes a contemplative thinker who seeks to understand the reason for human existence. He says, "I think us here to wonder, myself. To wonder. To ast. And that in wondering bout the big things, and asking about the big things you learn about the little ones, almost by acident. But you never know nothing more bout the big things that you start out with. The more I wonder, he say, the more I love." As a patriarch Albert was unable to love.

Unlike Walker's fictional character Albert, most men are not compelled by circumstances beyond their control to change. Most men who are suffering a crisis of masculinity do not know where to turn to seek change. In the film *Antwone Fisher* (which is based on a true story), the troubled young black male expresses his crisis by saying, "I don't know what to do." A feminist future for men can enable transformation and healing. As advocates of feminism who seek to end sexism and sexist oppression, we must be willing to hear men speak their pain. Only when we courageously face male pain without turning away will we model for men the emotional awareness healing requires.

To heal, men must learn to feel again. They must learn to break the silence, to speak the pain. Often men, to speak the pain, first turn to the women in their lives and are refused a hearing. In many ways women have bought into the patriarchal masculine mystique. Asked to witness a male expressing feelings, to listen to those feelings and respond, they may simply turn away. There was a time when I would often ask the man in my life to tell me his feelings. And yet when he began to speak, I would either interrupt or silence him by crying, sending him the message that his feelings were too heavy for anyone to bear, so it was best if he kept them to himself. As the *Sylvia* cartoon I have previously mentioned reminds us, women are fearful of hearing men voice feelings. I did not want to hear the pain of my male partner because hearing it required that I surrender my investment in the patriarchal ideal of the male as protector of the wounded. If he was wounded, then how could he protect me?

As I matured, as my feminist consciousness developed to include the recognition of patriarchal abuse of men, I could hear male pain. I could see men as comrades and fellow travelers on the journey of life and not as existing merely to provide instrumental support. Since men have yet to organize a feminist men's movement that would proclaim the rights of men to emotional awareness and expression, we will not know how many men have indeed tried to express feelings, only to have the women in their lives tune out or be turned off. Talking with men, I have been stunned when individual males would confess to sharing intense feelings with a male buddy, only to have that buddy either interrupt to silence the sharing, offer no response, or distance himself. Men of all ages who want to talk about feelings usually learn not to go to other men. And if they are heterosexual, they are far more likely to try sharing with women they have been sexually intimate with. Women talk about the fact that intimate conversation with males often takes place in the brief moments before and after sex. And of course our mass media provide the image again and again of the man who goes to a sex worker to share his feelings because there is no intimacy in that relationship and therefore no real emotional risk.

Being "vulnerable" is an emotional state many men seek to avoid. Some men spend a lifetime in a state of avoidance and therefore never experience intimacy. Sadly, we have all colluded with the patriarchy by faking it with men, pretending levels of intimacy and closeness we do not feel. We tell men we love them when we feel we have absolutely no clue as to who they really are. We tell fathers we love them when we are terrified to share our perceptions of them, our fear that if we disagree, we will be cast out, excommunicated. In this way we all collude with patriarchal culture to make men feel they can have it all, that they can embrace patriarchal manhood and still hold their loved ones dear. In reality, the more patriarchal a man is, the more disconnected he must be from feeling. If he cannot feel, he cannot connect. If he cannot connect, he cannot be intimate.

Significantly, Terrence Real suggests that most men do not know what intimacy is, that the "one-up, one-down world of masculinity leaves little space for tenderness . . . one is either controlled or controlling, dominator or dominated." He shares the powerful insight that "when they speak of fearing intimacy, what they really mean is that they fear subjugation." This fear of subjugation is often triggered by the reality that boys parented by patriarchal women are controlled via their longing for maternal closeness. In maternal sadism, the manipulative woman exploits the boy's emotional vulnerability to bind him to her will, to subjugate him. This early experience resides at the heart of many a man's fear of being intimate with a grown woman. And it may explain why so many men in patriarchal culture seek intimacy with girls or women young enough to be their daughters.

There is little feminist discussion of maternal sadism in relation to boys because it has been difficult for feminist thinkers to find a language to name the power mothers wield over children in a patriarchal culture, where in the larger social context mothers are so powerless. Yet it may be that very powerlessness in relation to grown men in patriarchy that leads so many women to exert emotional power over boys in a damaging manner. For this reason single-parent homes where mothers are dysfunctional and maternal sadism abounds are as unhealthy a place to raise boys as dysfunctional two-parent homes, where maternal sadism is the norm. In the two-parent home, the boy child may be fortunate to have an adult male who serves to intervene against maternal sadism, who acts as an enlightened witness. Such intervention is absent in the single female-headed household.

Women are not inherently more loving than men; women may give care and still be emotionally abusive. There has been such a strong tendency in patriarchal culture to simply assume that women are loving and capable of being intimate, that female failure to acquire the relational skills that would make intimacy possible, often goes unnoticed. Most females are encouraged to learn relational skills, yet damaged self-esteem may prevent us from applying those skills in a healthy manner. If we are to begin to create a culture in which feminist masculinity can thrive, then women who mother will need to educate themselves for critical consciousness. In the near future we may hope to have more data to show us the ways boys fare better when they have loving parents, whether together or apart, who teach them how to be intimate. Meanwhile let us create the space where males who lack relational skills can learn them.

As Zukav and Francis boldly state in *The Heart of the Soul*, "Intimacy and the pursuit of external power—the ability to manipulate and control—are incompatible." Before most men can be intimate with others, they have to be intimate with themselves. They have to learn to feel and to be aware of their feelings. Men who mask feelings or suppress them simply do not want to feel the pain. Since emotional pain is the feeling that most males have covered up, numbed out, or closed off, the journey back to feeling is frequently through the portal of suffering. Much male rage covers up this place of suffering: this is the well-kept secret. Often when a female gets close to male pain, penetrating the male mask to see the emotional vulnerability beneath, she becomes a target for the rage.

Shame at emotional vulnerability is often what men who are closed down emotionally seek to hide. Since shaming is often used to socialize boys away from their feeling selves toward the patriarchal male mask, many grown men have an internal shaming voice. Studies indicate that patriarchal fathers are rarely killed by their children; mothers are murdered more, for the rage many males feel from father shaming is usually transferred to female authority figures. With females, especially, the wounded boy inside the man can rage with no fear of reprisals. The more intimate the relationship, the more likely she is to be both the target of the rage and the secret keeper, telling no one that he is addicted to rage. This is especially the case where the acting-out male is a son who is physically hitting a mother or weaker siblings. The violence of sons, especially adolescent boys, toward mothers is rarely talked about in our culture. Now that so many adult single men return home to live with female parents or never even leave, there is a growing problem of domestic discord, both emotional and physical, that is covered up.

Intimate terrorism in male-female couple relationships is identified as a problem, particularly emotional abuse. Yet very little is said about the intimate terrorism between adult children and parents. The recent film *The Piano Teacher* graphically showed the sadomasochistic violence that can exist between an adult child and a parent, assuming the form of both emotional and physical abuse. In this film the adults shown are female, and audiences are allowed to interpret what they see according to traditional sexist notions of female competition. Yet in real life there is tremendous emotional abuse happening in single mother/adult son relationships that is not named. Women in patriarchal culture are trained to cover up and hide male abuse, all the more so when the culprit is a son and the victim his mother. These situations of unhealthy intimacy exist because of our cultural failure to teach women and men what intimacy is. And as long as women remain the primary parental caregivers, we will have the lion's share of the responsibility for learning how to be intimate ourselves and sharing that knowledge with male and female children.

Learning how to be intimate is a relational skill that teaches us the value of self-knowledge. Offering a broader, more meaningful definition of intimacy than the old notion of simply being close and vulnerable to someone, Gary Zukav and Linda Francis state that you "create intimacy when you shift from the pursuit of external power—the ability to manipulate and control—to the pursuit of authentic power—the alignment of your personality with your soul." In recent years there have been a number of self-help books published that urge readers to care for their souls. Such books by James Hillman, Thomas Moore, and Gary Zukav have been national bestsellers. Ironically, these men speak of the necessity of caring for our souls as though the path to that care is the same for women and men. In the introduction to Thomas Moore's *Care of the Soul* he tells readers, "Fulfilling work, rewarding relationships, personal power, and relief from symptoms are all gifts of the soul. They are particularly elusive in our time because we don't believe in the soul and therefore give it no place in our hierarchy of values. . . . We live in a time of deep division, in which mind is separated from body and spirituality is at odds with materialism. But how do we get out of this split?" Visionary thinkers believe that by exposing the way the logic of domination has created the split and choosing the model of interbeing and interdependency, we can begin the work of restoring integrity, and with integrity comes care of the soul.

Men caught up in the logic of patriarchal masculinity have difficulty believing that their souls matter. It is perhaps a patriarchal bias that leads Thomas Moore to suggest at the conclusion of his clarion call for all of us to cultivate soulfulness that "care of the soul is not a project of self-improvement. . . . It is not at all concerned with living properly or with emotional health." This need to deny the relationship of care of the soul to self-nurturance is itself indicative of the very binary splits in consciousness Moore critiques. There is no one who cares for her or his soul rightly who does not experience an enhancement of emotional well-being.

Men need to hear that their souls matter and that the care of their souls is the primary task of their being. Were all men seeking to uncover greater soulfulness in their lives rather than seeking power through a dominator model, then the world as we know it would be transformed for the better.

It cannot be a mere accident of fate that the visionary male teachers who are offering us messages about ways to care for the soul that will enhance life on the planet are men of color from poor countries, men who live in exile, men who have been victimized by imperialist male violence. Two men who come to mind are His Holiness the Dalai Lama and the Vietnamese Buddhist monk Thich Nhat Hanh. In *Ethics for the New Millennium* the Dalai Lama calls for a spiritual revolution. He shares his belief that all humans desire happiness and that a principal characteristic of genuine happiness is inner peace, which he links to developing concern for others. His soulful message echoes that of feminist thinkers who are telling the world that men can heal their spirits by developing relational skills—the ability to experience empathy, to care for others.

The existence of visionary male teachers who offer males and females spiritual guidance is a constant reminder to us that the hearts of men are transformed by love and compassion. Consistently, the Dalai Lama teaches us about the need to cultivate the practice of compassion. Whether males ever see themselves as working to end patriarchy, the fact remains that any man who chooses the way of compassion heals the spirit and moves away from domination. The Dalai Lama offers this wisdom:

> Compassion is one of the principal things that make our lives meaningful. It is the source of all lasting happiness and joy. And it is the foundation of a good heart. Through kindness, through affection, through honesty, through truth and justice toward all others we ensure our own benefit. This is not a matter for complicated theorizing. It is a matter of common sense. . . . There is no denying that our happiness is inextricably bound up with the happiness of others. There is no denying that if society suffers, we ourselves suffer. . . . Thus we can reject everything else: religion, ideology, all received wisdom. But we cannot escape the necessity of love and compassion.

This is the care of the soul that males and females must attend to if we are to sustain life on the planet, if we are to live fully and well.

Most men in our society believe in higher powers, and yet they have learned to devalue spiritual life, to violate their own sense of the sacred. Hence the work of spiritual restoration—of seeing the souls of men as sacred—is essential if we are to create a culture in which men can love. When the hearts of men are full of compassion and open to love, then, as the Dalai Lama states, "there is no need for temple or church, for mosque or synagogue, no need for complicated philosophy, doctrine or dogma, for our own heart, our own mind, is the temple and the doctrine is compassion."

When contemporary feminist movement was at its most militant, those of us who worshipped male deities were often made to feel as though we were traitors. Yet many of us found it especially useful in maintaining our love for males and appreciation for the sacredness of the male soul to separate patriarchal ideology from the powerful images of nurturing and loving kindness embodied in male religious figures. Many of us who were wounded daughters from Christian backgrounds found it useful to meditate daily on the twenty-third psalm because it evoked for us the image of a father caring for our souls, affirming and assuring us that we would survive, that goodness and mercy would be accorded us and that the father would keep us forever in his care.

This image of loving fatherhood embodies feminist masculinity in its most divine form. Healing the spirit, caring for the souls of boys and men, we must dare to proclaim our adoration, to bow down not to the male as dominator, but to the male as embodied divine spirit with whom we can unite in love, with no threat of separation, knowing a perfect love that is without fear.

10

Reclaiming Male Integrity

Healing the crisis in the hearts of men requires of us all a willingness to face the fact that patriarchal culture has required of men that they be divided souls. We know that there are men who have not succumbed to this demand but that most men have surrendered their capacity to be whole. The quest for integrity is the heroic journey that can heal the masculinity crisis and prepare the hearts of men to give and receive love.

Learning to wear a mask (that word already embedded in the term "masculinity") is the first lesson in patriarchal masculinity that a boy learns. He learns that his core feelings cannot be expressed if they do not conform to the acceptable behaviors sexism defines as male. Asked to give up the true self in order to realize the patriarchal ideal, boys learn self-betrayal early and are rewarded for these acts of soul murder. Therapist John Bradshaw explains the splitting that takes place when a child learns that the way he organically feels is not acceptable. In response to this lesson that his true self is inappropriate and wrong, the boy learns to don a false self. Bradshaw explains, "The feeling that I have done something wrong, that I really don't know what it is, that there's something terribly wrong with my very being, leads to a sense of utter hopelessness. This hopelessness is the deepest cut of the mystified state. It means there is no possibility for me as I am; there is no way I can matter or be worthy of anyone's love as long as I remain myself. I must find a way to be someone else—someone who is lovable. Someone who is not me." Sexist roles restrict the identity formation of male and female children, but the process is far more damaging to boys because not only are the roles required of them more rigid and confining, but they are much more likely to receive severe punishment when they deviate from these roles.

Contemporary feminist movement created a socially sanctioned space where girls can create a sense of self that is distinct from sexist definitions; the same freedom has not been extended to boys. No wonder then that boys in patriarchal culture continue the tradition of creating a false self, of being split. That split in boys and men is often characterized by the capacity to compartmentalize. It is this division in the psyches and souls of males, fundamentally wounding, that is the breeding ground for mental illness. When males are required to wear the mask of a false self, their capacity to live fully and freely is severely diminished. They cannot experience joy and they can never truly love.

Anyone who has a false self must be dishonest. People who learn to lie to themselves and others cannot love because they are crippled in their capacity to tell the truth and therefore unable to trust. This is the heart of the psychological damage done to men in patriarchy. It is a form of abuse that this culture continues to deny. Boys socialized to become patriarchs are being abused. As victims of child abuse via socialization in the direction of the patriarchal ideal, boys learn that they are unlovable. According to Bradshaw they learn that "relationships are based on power, control, secrecy, fear, shame, isolation, and distance." These are the traits often admired in the patriarchal adult man.

Emotionally wounding boys is socially acceptable and even demanded in patriarchal culture. Denying them their right to be whole, to have integrity, is not only encouraged, it is seen as the right way to do things. Terrence Real says that "we force our children out of the wholeness and connectedness in which they begin their lives" and then encourage them "to bury their deepest selves, to stop speaking, or attending to the truth, to hold in mistrust, or even in disdain, the state of closeness we all, by our natures, most crave." Exposing the harsh reality of the psychological impact of patriarchy, Real has the courage to speak this truth: "We live in an antirelational, vulnerability-despising culture, one that not only fails to nurture the skills of connection but actively fears them." Teaching boys to despise their vulnerability is one way to socialize them to engage in self-inflicted soul murder. This wound in the male spirit, caused by learned acts of splitting, of disassociation and disconnection, can only be healed by the practice of integrity. Wounded males must recover all the parts of the self they abandoned in serving the needs of patriarchal maleness. Such recovery is the necessary groundwork for restoring integrity to male being.

Speaking about the meaning of integrity in his most recent book, *Living a Life That Matters,* Rabbi Harold Kushner offers this clear definition: "Integrity means being whole, unbroken, undivided. It describes a person who has united the different parts of his or her personality, so that there is no longer a split in the soul." Patriarchy encourages men to surrender their integrity and to live lives of denial. By learning the arts of compartmentalization, dissimulation, and disassociation, men are able to see themselves as acting with integrity in cases where they are not. Their learned state of psychological denial is severe. Adding to the definition of integrity in *Further along the Road Less Traveled,* M. Scott Peck discusses the root meaning of the term "integrity," which is the verb "to integrate," emphasizing that this is the opposite of compartmentalization. "Individuals without integrity naturally compartmentalize. And patriarchal masculinity normalizes male compartmentalization."

Peck argues that compartmentalization is a way to avoid feeling pain: "We're all familiar with the man who goes to church on Sunday morning, believing that he loves God and God's creation and his fellow human beings, but who, on Monday morning, has no trouble with his company's policy of dumping toxic wastes in the local stream. He can do this because he has religion in one compartment and his business in another." Since most men have been socialized to believe that compartmentalization is a positive practice, it feels right, it feels comfortable. To practice integrity, then, is difficult; it hurts. Peck makes the crucial point: "Integrity is painful. But without it there can be no wholeness." To be whole men must practice integrity.

Integrity is needed for healthy self-esteem. Most males have low self-esteem because they are constantly lying and dissimulating (taking on false appearances) in order to perform the sexist male role. Identifying the practice of integrity as a core pillar of self-esteem in his groundbreaking work on the subject, *Six Pillars of Self-Esteem,* Nathaniel Branden talks about the way in which lying wounds self-esteem. He confesses that, like many men, he once convinced himself that it was important to tell lies to protect other people, but eventually he had to face the truth that "lies do not work." To honor his self-esteem, to practice integrity, he learned that the truth had to be told, that "by procrastinating and delaying I merely made the consequences for everyone more terrible." Furthermore, he writes, "I succeeded in protecting no one, least of all myself. If part of my motive was to spare people I cared about, I inflicted a worse pain than they would otherwise have experienced. If part of my motive was to protect my self-esteem by avoiding a conflict among my values and loyalties, it was my self-esteem that I damaged." This faulty logic he describes is the same that many patriarchal men use to avoid telling the truth and practicing integrity.

All too often we are led to believe that men gain more power through lying and compartmentalization. It just simply is not so. The stress of guarding and protecting a false self is harmful to male emotional well-being; it erodes self-esteem. Much of the depression men suffer is directly related to their inability to be whole. Even though they have been socialized to create and maintain false selves, most men remember the true self that once existed. And it is that memory of loss—coupled with rage at the world, which encouraged the surrender of the self—that engenders depression. This suffering, the source of which often goes unidentified in adult males, is constant. It leads many men to addiction, whether to workaholism or substance abuse.

Workaholism is the most common addiction in men because it is usually rewarded and not taken seriously as detrimental to their emotional well-being.

Work is often the space where men detach from feelings. Zukav and Francis describe workaholism as a flight from emotions: "It is a drug that is as effective as the most powerful anesthetic. . . . Workaholism is a deep sleep. It is a self-induced trance that temporarily keeps painful emotions away from your awareness." At the moment when addictions stop keeping the pain at bay, many men sink into depression. And as with so much male pain, it is only in recent years that men have been given societal permission to confront depression. Men suffer depression frequently because of their own unfulfilled expectations or their perfectionism (which can never be satisfied since to be human is to be imperfect). Often it is suggested that feminist movement has taken away or undermined "male power," and as a consequence, men feel bereft. Underlying this notion is the idea that women are to blame for male depression, although it is difficult to believe that men feel at all threatened by masses of women entering a workforce where they receive less pay than men and come home after long hours to do a second shift. Since a woman outside the home is no longer under the rule of the individual patriarchal head of household, this movement outside may threaten male power more than what women do on the outside.

One dimension of feminist movement that did have a profound impact on men was its insistence that women had the right to critique men both collectively and individually. In the patriarchal home I was raised in, a significant aspect of Dad's power was that he was beyond critique. Even though Mom never became a feminist, after forty years of submission she did begin to critique Dad in ways that echoed feminist challenges to male power and privilege. Like many women, she challenged her husband's lack of emotional engagement. Like many women, she has wanted him to be interested in personal growth. For years patriarchal culture has taught men that their selfhood, their manhood, is affirmed by a lack of interest in personal growth; all of a sudden in the wake of feminist movement, women were bombarding men with new emotional expectations. Collectively men responded with a feeling of depression.

Popular psychotherapist M. Scott Peck reminds us that anytime any of us takes significant steps to grow, we go through a process of denial, anger, bargaining, depression, and acceptance (the same stages Elisabeth Kübler-Ross identified as those we go through when we confront dying). He gives the example of his being criticized for character flaws by loved ones and resisting the critique:

> If they truly do love me enough to keep on criticizing, then maybe I get to the point where I think, "Could they be right? Could there possibly be something wrong with the great Scott Peck?" And if I answer yes, then that's depressing. But if I can hang in there with that depressing notion—that maybe there really is something wrong with me—and start to wonder what it might be, if I contemplate it and analyze it and isolate it, and identify it, then I can go about the process of

> killing it and purifying myself of it. Having done—fully completed—the work of depression, I will then emerge at the other end as a new man, a resurrected human being, a better person.

Often, however, men find themselves stuck in the place of rage.

No wonder then that many men seeking to be whole must first name the intensity of their rage and the pain it masks. Writing in the face of the knowledge that he is dying, Joseph Beam confesses in "Brother to Brother: Words from the Heart":

> What is most important to me must be spoken, made verbal and shared, even at the risk of having it bruised or misunderstood. I know anger. My body contains as much anger as water. It is the material from which I have built my house: blood red bricks that cry in the rain. . . . It is the face and posture I show the world. It is the way, sometimes the only way, I am granted an audience. It is sometimes the way I show affection. I am angry because of the treatment I am afforded as a Black man. That fiery anger is stoked with the fuels of contempt and despisal shown me by my community because I am gay. I cannot go home as I am.

Anger often hides depression and profound sorrow.

Depression often masks the inability to grieve. Males are not given the emotional space to grieve. Girls and women can cry, can express sorrow throughout our lives. We can just let it out. Males are still being taught to keep it in and, worse, to deny that they feel like crying. Donald Dutton in his chapter "Love and Rage" says that male refusal to acknowledge loss is a key component of male rage:

> Male models for grieving are few. . . . Men in particular seem incapable of grieving and mourning on an individual basis. Perhaps that is why the blues are so popular with men. They serve a socially sanctioned form of expression for this lost and unattainable process. . . . When blues artist Robert Johnson sings, "I've been mistreated and I don't mind dying," a multitude of men can feel their own unmet yearnings and nod in assent.

Many adolescent girls go through a grieving process as they make the transition from being a small child to mature girlhood. Girls are allowed to mourn changes. Males have no rituals of mourning, as boys or men.

One of the reasons the church has been so important in the lives of black men is that it is one of the locations where they are allowed to express emotions, where they can grieve. James Baldwin describes this release of emotions in church in *The Fire Next Time*: "Nothing that has happened to me since equals the power and the glory that I sometimes felt when, in the middle of a sermon, I knew that I was somehow, by some miracle, really carrying, as they said, 'the Word'—when the church and I were one. Their pain and their joy were mine, and mine were theirs—they surrendered their joy to me, I surrendered mine to them." It was in the church of my childhood that I first saw men mourn.

To grow psychologically and spiritually, men need to mourn. The men who are doing the work of self-recovery testify that it is only when they are able to feel the pain that they can begin to heal. With courage and insight Neale Lundgren speaks about this inner struggle in his autobiographical essay about boyhood, "The Night When Sleep Awoke," confessing his longing to find a father model, to reconnect with manhood. "Just when I thought I had exhausted my search for the father, I began to reach out for therapeutic help. After several episodes of chronic, unexplainable depression, I made a decision to finally stop avoiding the hurt and anger. With assistance and support from therapeutically literate men and women, I began to explore the feared terrain of my wounded heart. I began to grieve past losses and attachments." When a man's emotional capacity to mourn is arrested, he is likely to be frozen in time and unable to complete the process of growing up. Men need to mourn the old self and create the space for a new self to be born if they are to change and be wholly transformed.

If a man is not willing to break patriarchal rules that say that he should never change—especially to satisfy someone else, particularly a female—then he will choose being right over being loved. He will turn away from loved ones and choose his manhood over his personhood, isolation over connectedness. Therapist George Edmond Smith remembers learning early that men will respond with rage and rejection if they are perceived to be out of control or making a mistake:

> I also recall early in life that when I asked my father a question to which he did not know the answer, he became angry, as if to say, "Look, I don't know the answer to your question and because of that I should kick your ass!" Of course, I realized this almost immediately and I stopped looking to my father for answers. Perhaps if he had taken the time to say to me, "Son, I don't know the answer to that, let's look it up together and find out."

Only a father capable of being whole can have the integrity to acknowledge ignorance to his son without feeling diminished.

Men who are whole can speak their fear without shame. They do not need to wear the false mask of fearlessness. Fathers have been unable to share with their sons that they are afraid. They fear not measuring up to the expectations of sons. They fear that the son will see their jealousy and envy of the boy who has not yet severed his relation to feeling, who is not emotionally closed off. Writing about his boyhood, Neale Lundgren recalls, "I was in awe of my father, and it seemed to me that I often sensed he was afraid of me. Perhaps he was intimidated by my heart that was as his used to be when he was a boy: big, full, open, strong, and tender."

Unable to acknowledge feelings, fathers often cover them up with rage, cruelly severing their own attachment to the son and refusing his love and admiration. The competitive performance model of patriarchy teaches men who father that a son is or will be his adversary, that he has to fear the son's stealing his glory. Our myths and religious stories are full of narratives in which the son is depicted as the father's enemy, ever poised to steal his power. The dysfunctional model suggests to men that separation can only be forged through violence and death. Only the man who chooses a healthy model—wherein the father figure, the adult man of integrity, the guide who shelters, protects, and nurtures the son—can gracefully attend the assertion of his own son's healthy autonomy.

When father figures are healthy, they know when to let go; they can affirm the boy every step of the way. As Thomas Moore declares in his essay about boyhood, "Little Boy Found," "If the fathers speak to us, we can preserve our golden spirits. . . . Fathers and sons need each other, for they sustain each other. We need to let our fathers be slow to grow up. . . . They need to take our childlike foolishness seriously, giving their lives for it, so that we can be fathers ourselves from our place in the sun." Caring fathers with bold strength and integrity shield the open, tender hearts of their sons, protecting them from patriarchy's hard-hearted assaults.

When men practice integrity, they accept that part of the work of wholeness is learning to be flexible, learning how to negotiate, how to embrace change in thought and action. The ability to critique oneself and change and to hear critique from others is the condition of being that makes us capable of responsibility.

To be able to respond to family and friends, men have to have practice assuming responsibility. This is another component of healthy self-esteem. Nathaniel Brandon equates our capacity to be responsible with our capacity to experience joy, to be personally empowered. This sense of personal agency lets us break with imposed sex roles. This is true freedom and independence:

> I am responsible for accepting or choosing the values by which I live. If I live by values I have accepted or adopted passively and unthinkingly, it is easy to imagine that they are just "my nature," just "who I am," and to avoid recognizing that choice is involved. If I am willing to recognize that choices and decisions are crucial when values are adopted, then I can take a fresh look at my values, question them, and if necessary revise them. Again, it is taking responsibility that sets me free.

The patriarchal model that tells men that they must be in control at all times is at odds with cultivating the capacity to be responsible, which requires knowing when to control and when to surrender and let go.

Responsible men are capable of self-criticism. If more men were doing the work of self-critique, then they would not be wounded, hurt, or chagrined when critiqued by others, especially women with whom they are intimate. Engaging in self-critique empowers responsible males to admit mistakes. When they have wronged others, they are willing to acknowledge wrongdoing and make amends. When others have wronged them, they are able to forgive. The ability to be forgiving is part of letting go of perfectionism and accepting vulnerability.

At the same time, constructive criticism works only

when it is linked to a process of affirmation. Giving affirmation is an act of emotional care. Wounded men are not often able to say anything positive. They are the grump-and-groan guys; cloaked in cynicism, they stand at an emotional distance from themselves and others. Affirmation brings us closer together. It is the highest realization of compassion and empathy with others. One of the negative aspects of antimale feminist critiques of masculinity was the absence of any affirmation of that which is positive and potentially positive in male being. When individuals, including myself, wrote about the necessity of affirming men and identifying them as comrades in struggle, we were often labeled male-identified. The women who attacked us did not understand that it was possible to critique patriarchy without hating men. Indeed, recognizing all the ways that males have been victimized by patriarchy (even though they received rewards) was a way of including men in feminist movement, welcoming their presence and honoring their contribution.

Critical analysis is useful when it promotes growth, but it is never enough. The work of affirmation is what brings us together. When men learn to affirm themselves and others, giving this soul care, then they are on the path to wholeness. When men are able to do little acts of mercy, they can be in communion with others without the need to dominate. No longer separate, no longer apart, they bring a wholeness that can be joined with the wholeness of others. This is interbeing. As whole people they can experience joy. Unlike happiness, joy is a lasting state that can be sustained even when everything is not the way we want it to be. In the essay "Celebrating Life" Jesuit priest Henri Nouwen declares that "where there is joy there is life." Nouwen left his prestigious professorships at Ivy League schools to work in a community for the mentally handicapped. As spiritual guide and hands-on caretaker, he found his integrity affirmed through the act of serving others. Therapist George Edmond Smith in *Walking Proud: Black Men Living beyond the Stereotypes* testifies that his psychological growth was enhanced when he began "doing very simple things that are unselfish." He tells readers that if men "would commit to good and not evil during each waking moment, their lives would change dramatically."

Men of integrity are not ashamed to serve. They are caretakers, guardians, keepers of the flame. They know joy. I have written in praise of my grandfather, the man who loved me in my childhood consistently and unconditionally, in the memoir of my growing up, *Bone Black:* "His smells fill my nostrils with the scent of happiness. With him all the broken bits and pieces of my heart come together again." This is the true meaning of reunion, living the knowledge that the damage can be repaired, that we can be whole again. It is the ultimate fulfillment that comes when men dare to challenge and change patriarchy.

11

Loving Men

Growing up, I knew my father as the strong man who did not talk, who did not show feelings, who did not give time or attention. He was the provider, the protector, the warrior guarding the gate. He was the stranger in the house. We were not allowed to know him, to hear his boyhood stories, to revel in his memories. His life was shrouded in mystery. We searched for him. Standing in front of the photos of him as a young soldier, of him as a boxer, Dad at the pool hall in his glory, Dad on the basketball court. We stood in front of the photo of the all-black infantry unit he served in during World War II. A favorite game of our childhood was to find Dad in the photo, our father, the quintessential patriarch—a man of his times, raised for war.

To write about men and love, I must speak of war. Time and time again we have been told that civilization cannot survive men's loving, for if men love, they will not be able to kill on command. However, if men were natural-born killers, hardwired by biology and destiny to take life, then there would be no need for patriarchal socialization to turn them into killers. The warrior's way wounds boys and men; it has been the arrow shot through the heart of their humanity. The warrior's way has led men in the direction of an impoverishment of spirit so profound that it threatens all life on planet Earth.

Writing about his boyhood and the warrior way, in the essay "My War Story" Shepherd Bliss openly confesses that he is "a child of trauma, a specific kind of trauma—military trauma, war trauma." Having grown up in the military, become a soldier, then having grown into an advocate of peace, Bliss takes a stand against war and the warrior's way:

> The warrior ethic has damaged us. As we move into the twenty-first century we need to mature beyond war and warriors. I disagree with those men's movement writers and activists who speak so highly of the warrior. I appreciate some of his traits—like courage, teamwork, loyalty—but the archetype itself is bankrupt at this point in history. We surely need guardians, boundary-setters, husbandmen, and citizens. If we are to survive on this planet, so threatened by war and warriors, we must get beyond the obsolete archetype of the warrior and value images such as the peacemaker, the partner, and the husbandman who cares for the earth and animals.

Even though war is failing as a strategy for sustaining life and creating safety, our nation's leaders force us into battle, giving new life to the dying patriarchy.

War was in its earliest forms inclusive of women and men. Detailing its history in *Blood Rites,* Barbara Ehrenreich reminds us that "by assigning the triumphant predator status to males alone, humans have helped themselves to 'forget' that nightmarish prehistory in which they were, male and female, prey to larger, stronger animals. . . . Gender, in other words, is an idea that coincidentally obliterates our common past as prey, and states that the predator status is innate and 'natural'—at least to men." Calling attention to the fact that war has been not simply a male occupation but rather "an activity that has often served to define manhood itself," Ehrenreich argues that "warfare and aggressive masculinity" are mutually reinforcing. The gendered nature of war makes men predators and women prey. We cannot speak of men and love, of love between women and men, without speaking of the need to bring an end to war and all thinking that makes war possible.

The slogan "Make love not war" was popular at that moment in our nation's history when individual males were most conscious of their need to resist patriarchal masculinity. It is no accident that Daniel Berrigan, imprisoned for antiwar activities, would talk with Thich Nhat Hanh about the need for solidarity, for everyone to learn how to make community. These two men of integrity talk together in *The Raft Is Not the Shore* about the need for communities of resistance. Thich Nhat Hanh says:

> And resistance, at root, I think must mean more than resistance against war. It is a resistance against all kinds of things that are like war. Because living in modern society, one feels that he cannot easily retain integrity, wholeness. One is robbed permanently of humanness, the capacity of being oneself. . . . So perhaps, first of all,

> resistance means opposition to being invaded, occupied, assaulted, and destroyed by the system. The purpose of resistance, here, is to seek the healing of yourself in order to be able to see clearly. . . . Communities of resistance should be places where people can return to themselves more easily, where the conditions are such that they can heal themselves and recover their wholeness.

Berrigan asks that relationships, committed partnerships, be seen as vital communities of resistance.

In dominator cultures most families are not safe places. Dysfunction, intimate terrorism, and violence make them breeding grounds for war. Since we have yet to end patriarchal culture, our struggles to end domination must begin where we live, in the communities we call home. It is there that we experience our power to create revolutions, to make life-transforming change. We already know that men do not have to remain wedded to patriarchy. Individual men have again and again staked a different claim, claiming their rights to life and love. They are beacons of hope embodying the truth that men can love.

If we are to create a culture in which all males can learn to love, we must first reimagine family in all its diverse forms as a place of resistance. We must be willing to see boyhood differently, not as a time when boys are indoctrinated into a manhood that is about violence and death but rather as a time when boys learn to glory in the connection with others, in the revelry and joy of intimacy that is the essential human longing. We should follow the wisdom of

Thomas Moore when he calls for nonpatriarchal adoration of the boy:

> What a mystery it is to be a boy, so close to death and birth, so uneducated and therefore so fresh and uncynical. We should end our disparagement of the boy, of our own immaturities, of our tardiness in growing up, of our sheer delight in beauty, of our love of the sun, of our vertical inclinations, and of our wanderings and great falls. . . . We could speak words of encouragement to this boy where we find him—in our friends and students, in our institutions, and in our own hearts. If we do not speak to him in this way, he will be lost, and we will have lost with him, all tenderness and grace.

To create the culture that will enable boys to love, we must see the family as having as its primary function the giving of love (providing food and shelter are loving acts).

Learning how to love in family life, boys (and girls) learn the relational skills needed to build community at home and in the world. Poet Wendell Berry speaks of such a movement as a return to a respect for the innate holiness of all beings:

> If we are lucky enough as children to be surrounded by grown-ups who love us, then our sense of wholeness is not just the sense of completeness in ourselves but also is the sense of belonging to others and to our place; it is an

> unconscious awareness of community, of having in common. It may be that this double sense of singular integrity and of communal belonging is our personal standard of health for as long as we live . . . we seem to know instinctively that health is not divided.

When our families are functional and not shaped by a dominator model and the patriarchal thinking that comes in its wake, the model of health Berry describes can become the norm.

In such a world boys may think of games that do not center around the causing of pain, the creation of death, but will indeed be forms of play that celebrate life and wholeness. And the individual differences that arise between boys, and between boys and girls, will not need to be interpreted as a cause for domination, for one to rule over the other, but will become occasions for exploration, for the sharing of knowledge and the invention of new ways of being. Loving parents already see that if rigid gender roles are not imposed on boys, they will make their decisions about selfhood in relation to their passions, their longings, their gifts. We cannot honor boys rightly, protecting their emotional lives, without ending patriarchy. To pretend otherwise is to collude with the ongoing soul murder that is enacted in the name of turning boys into men.

Without a doubt there will always be boys who will choose activities that are rambunctious, that call for physical strength and require an element of risk, but there will also be boys who will seek quieter pleasures, who will turn away from risk. There will be boys whose personalities will be somewhere in between these two paradigms. If boys are raised to be empathic and strong; autonomous and connected; responsible to self, to family and friends, and to society; able to make community rooted in a recognition of interbeing, then the solid foundation is present and they will be able to love.

To make this solid foundation, men must set the example by daring to heal, by daring to do the work of relational recovery. Irrespective of their sexual preferences, men in the process of self-recovery usually begin by returning to boyhood and evaluating what they learned about masculinity and how they learned it. Many males find it useful to pinpoint the moments when they realized who they were, what they felt, then suppressed that knowledge because it was displeasing to others. Understanding the roots of male dis-ease helps many men begin the work of repairing the damage. Progressive individual gay men in our nation, particularly those who have resisted patriarchal thinking (who are often labeled "feminine" for being emotionally aware), have been at the forefront of relational recovery. Straight men and patriarchal gay men can learn from them.

Men are on the path to love when they choose to become emotionally aware. Zukav and Francis see this as a process: "Emotional awareness is more than applying techniques to this circumstance or that circumstance. It is a natural expression of an orientation that turns your attention toward the most noble, fulfilling, joyful, and empowering part of yourselves that you can reach for. That is your soul." Women want men to be more emotionally aware. This is especially so for women who want to be in loving partnerships with men. Yet just as there is a crisis for men, women are experiencing a crisis of faith where men are concerned. The form that crisis takes is despair about the capacity of men to make constructive change, to achieve emotional maturity, to grow up.

The notion that lesbian women are antimale always proves false when groups of women gather and talk about men. The most vicious man-hating comments are always made by women who are with men and who plan to be with them for the rest of their lives. After forty-nine years of marriage, my mother is angry with our dad. The perfect subordinated wife, now when they are both over seventy years in age, is upset that he is not more emotionally giving. Since she is not a feminist, she does not see that it is a contradiction to expect this old-time patriarch to suddenly give her love. Her anger surprises and enrages him. Mama's anger masks her fear that any day now she could die without ever feeling loved by the man she has devoted her entire life to pleasing. Like the men who feel that patriarchy's promise has not been fulfilled, Mama feels that she is left with broken promises, without the reward for performing the subordinate role she was told a good woman should perform.

Women who are not feminist, women who support patriarchy, who do not have problems with sexism, share with their feminist, antisexist counterparts the wish that men would be more loving. Shere Hite documented this longing in her massive study *Women and Love: A Cultural Revolution In Progress.* Her chapter "Loving Men at This Time in History" begins with the observation that "strangely, hauntingly, most women in this study—whether married, single, or divorced, of all ages—say they have not yet found the love they are looking for." The love women are looking for in relationships with men is one based on mutuality in partnership. Mutuality is different from equality.

Women once believed that men would give us more respect if we showed we were their equals. In a world where gender inequality is for most people an accepted norm, men withhold from women their respect. The root of the word "respect" means "to look at." Women want to be recognized, seen, and cared about by the men in our lives. We desire respect whether gender equality exists in all areas or not. When a woman and man have promised to give each other love, to be mutually supportive, to bring together care, commitment, knowledge, respect, responsibility, and trust, even if there are circumstances of inequality, no one uses that difference to enforce domination. Love cannot coexist with domination. Love can exist in circumstances where equality is not the order of the day. Inequality, in and of itself, does not breed domination. It can heighten awareness of the need to be more loving.

Many women despair of men because they believe that ultimately men care more about being dominators than they do about being loving partners. They believe this because so many men refuse to make the changes that would make mutual love possible. Women have not proven that they care enough about the hearts of men, about their emotional well-being, to challenge patriarchy on behalf of those men with whom they want to know love. We read self-help books that tell us all the time that we cannot change anyone, and this is a useful truism. It is however equally true that when we give love, real love—not the emotional exchange of I will give you what you want if you give me what I want, but genuine care, commitment, knowledge, responsibility, respect, and trust—it can serve as the seductive catalyst for change. Any woman who supports patriarchy who then claims to either love the men in her life or be frustrated that they do not love her is in a state of denial.

Women who want men to love know that that cannot really happen without a revolution of consciousness where men stop patriarchal thinking and action. Because sexist roles have always given women support for emotional development, it has been easier for women to find our way to love. We do not love better or more than men, but we do find it easier to get in touch with feelings because even patriarchal society supports this trait in us. Men will never receive support from patriarchal culture for their emotional development. But if as enlightened witnesses we offer the men we love (our fathers, brothers, lovers, friends, comrades) affirmation that they can change as well as assurance that we will accept them when they are changed, transformation will not seem as risky.

As individual men have become more aware of the lovelessness in their lives, they have also recognized their longing for love. This recognition does not mean that men know what to do. Importantly, when men love, it changes the nature of their sexuality, both how they think about sex and how they perform sexually. Many men fear learning to love because they cannot imagine a sexuality beyond the patriarchal model. In a world where men love, a focus on eros and eroticism will naturally replace male obsession with sex. All men could have the opportunity to enjoy sexual pleasure, and that includes sexual fantasy, for its own sake and not as a substitute for fantasies of domination or as a way to assert manhood in place of selfhood, were they taught a healthy eroticism.

Often men use perverse sexual fantasy (particularly the consumption of patriarchal pornography) as a hiding place for depression and grief. Patriarchal pornography is the place where men can pretend that the promise of patriarchal power can always be fulfilled. Michael Kimmel explores this aspect of male lust in his essay "Fuel for Fantasy": "The pornographic utopia is a world of abundance, abandon, and autonomy—a world, in short, utterly unlike the one we inhabit. . . . Most men don't feel especially good about themselves, living lives of 'quiet desperation.' . . . Pornographic fantasy is a revenge against the real world of men's lives. To transform those fantasies requires that we also transform that reality." Transforming the real world men inhabit requires our collective will to dream anew the male body and being as a site of beauty, pleasure, desire, and human possibility. In *The Soul of Sex* James Hillman declares:

> One of the first achievements to be made in the reconciliation of body and spirit, which is a prerequisite for a deepened, soul-filled sexuality, is a rediscovery of the virtue and value of the body's eroticism. . . . To find the soul of sex we have to wrench it out of the materialistic and mechanistic body that we have created by means of our modern philosophies and reunite it with the subtle, fantasy-filled, mythologized body of the imagination.

Damaged in that openhearted place where they could imagine freely, men must undergo a healing restoration of the will to imagine before they can break with a model of sexuality that breeds addiction while denying them access to a sexuality that satisfies.

Steve Bearman explains male compulsion for sex as interrupted eros in his essay "Why Men Are So Obsessed with Sex":

> Directly and indirectly, we are handed sexuality as the one vehicle through which it might still be possible to express and experience essential aspects of our humanness that have been slowly and systematically conditioned out of us. Sex was, and is, presented as the road to real intimacy, complete closeness, as the arena in which it is okay to openly love, to be tender and vulnerable and yet remain safe, to not feel so deeply alone. Sex is the one place sensuality seems to be permissible, where we can be gentle with our own bodies and allow ourselves our overflowing passion. Pleasure and desire, vitality and excitement seemingly left behind somewhere we can't even remember, again become imaginable.

Poignant and powerfully evocative, this is the promise of sexuality within patriarchy, but it is a promise that ultimately can never be fulfilled. Men and boys who embrace it are doomed to be forever yearning, forever in a state of lack.

Bearman makes the point that after being taught to be obsessed with sex via patriarchal conditioning, males are "then subjected to continuous conditioning to repress sensuality, numb feelings, ignore our bodies, and separate from our natural closeness with human beings." He continues, "All of these human needs are then promised to us by way of sex and sexuality.... But in no way can sex completely fulfill these needs. Such needs can only be fulfilled by healing from the effects of male conditioning and suffusing every area of our lives with relatedness and aliveness." Suggesting that men resist repression and choose passion as they reclaim their feeling lives, Bearman identifies passion as the "greatest ally" men can choose in their efforts to liberate their complete humanity. The root meaning of the Latin word *patior* is "to suffer." To claim passion, men must embrace the pain, feel the suffering, moving through it to the world of pleasure that awaits. This is the heroic journey for men in our times. It is not a journey leading to conquest and domination, to disconnecting and cutting off life; it is a journey of reclamation where the bits and pieces of the self are found and put together again, made whole.

As men work to be whole, sex assumes its rightful place as one pleasure among many pleasures. Unlike addictive patriarchal sex, passion rooted in a life-affirming erotic ethos deepens emotional connection. According to Zukav and Francis:

> Loving sexual intimacy ... expresses care and appreciation. It is mutual giving, not mutual taking. It is an arena in which individuals nurture each other rather than exploit each other. In loving sexual intimacy, sexual partners are

> not interchangeable. They are unique in their histories, aptitudes, struggles, and joys. They know each other and care for each other. They empathize. They are interested in each other. They use physical intimacy to deepen their emotional intimacy.... They are committed to growing together.

Individual men who have found their way back to a restored sense of the erotic, to eros as a life force, need to share their bliss with men in general. Bearman tells us:

> My vision for myself and for all men is that we reclaim every piece of our humanity that has been denied us by our conditioning. Obsession with sex can be healed when we reclaim all the essential aspects of the human experience that we have learned to manage without: our affinity for one another, caring connections with people of all ages and backgrounds and genders, sensual enjoyment of our bodies, passionate self-expression, exhilarating desire, tender love for ourselves and for another, vulnerability, help with our difficulties, gentle rest, getting and staying close with many people in many kinds of relationships.

Women who love men share this vision.

We yearn for boys and men to find their way to self-love. We yearn for boys and men to move from self-love to healing fellowship with one another. No man who reclaims passion for his life fears the passion in another man. He is not homophobic, for to be so would be a rejection of the self-acceptance and acceptance of others that is essential to the formation and maintenance of self-esteem. If all men were in touch with primal positive passion, the categories of gay and straight would lose their charged significance.

In *A Queer Geography* Frank Browning makes the useful distinction between gay identity politics, which often closes down connection, and a commitment to eros and eroticism that widens connections:

> By erotic, I mean all the powerful attractions we might have: for mentoring and being mentored, for unrealizable flirtation, for intellectual tripping, for sweaty mateship at play or at work, for spiritual ecstasy, for being held in silent grief, for explosive rage at a common enemy, for the sublime love of friendship. All or none of these ways of loving might be connected to the fact that I usually have sex with men because all of these loves can and do happen with both men and women in my life.

Patriarchy has sought to repress and tame erotic passion precisely because of its power to draw us into greater and greater communion with ourselves, with those we know most intimately, and with the stranger.

Feminism changed the intimate lives of women and men by offering to everyone a vision of relationships rooted in mutuality, a vision of partnerships without domination. This seductive promise can be fulfilled only as patriarchal thinking ceases to dominate the consciousness of women and men, girls and boys. Seeking to heal the wounds inflicted by patriarchy, we have to go to the source. We have to look at males directly, eye to eye, and speak the truth that the time has come for males to have a revolution of values. We cannot turn our hearts away from boys and men, then ponder why the politics of war continues to shape our national policy and our intimate romantic lives.

There is a war between the sexes in this nation, between those who believe they are destined to be predators and those they deem prey. Resistance to gender domination has intensified that war. As feminist thinking and practice loses visibility, many females look to patriarchy for their salvation. More than ever before in our nation's history, females are encouraged to assume the patriarchal mask and bury their emotional selves as deeply as their male counterparts do. Females embrace this paradigm because they feel it is better to be a dominator than to be dominated. However, this is a perverse vision of gender equality that offers women equal access to the house of the dead. In that house there will be no love.

Most women have yet to collectively embrace the alternative theories and practices visionary thinkers—female and male but especially feminists—have offered to heal our wounded hearts and our suffering planet. Unlike most men, most women are taught relational skills. It is clear though that more often than not women have used those skills in the service of domination, of patriarchy, and not in the quest for freedom or love. Acknowledging this fact, we see that most women are not any more advanced than men as a group. In both groups individuals are seeking salvation, seeking wholeness, daring to be radical and revolutionary, but for the most part the great majority of folk are still uncertain about taking the path that will end gender warfare and make love possible. While it is evident that many men are not as willing to explore and follow the path that leads to self-recovery as are women, we cannot journey far if men are left behind. They wield too much power to be simply ignored or forgotten. Those of us who love men do not want to continue our journey without them. We need them beside us because we love them.

I share with Terrence Real the vision of relational recovery, which invites men who have been outside the circle of love to return. The male journey to love will never be easy or simple in patriarchal culture. Like women who have navigated difficult terrain to open our hearts, to find love, men need consciousness raising, support groups, therapy, education. Emotionally starved and shut down, males, sick with the pain of lovelessness, need loved ones to do positive interventions like those we are encouraged to make when addiction to substances is the issue. As Real states, "It is a tough antirelational world out there. The old terms have been with us for a very long time. We should expect to get caught up in them sometimes, losing our way. That's when help from those who know and love us is essential." Men seeking help often find it difficult to find support. We ask them to change without creating a culture of change to affirm and assist them.

Time and time again when I struggled to do the work of love with a male partner who was not changing, I was told to give up on him, to kick him to the curb. I was told I was wasting my time. All this negative feedback made me ponder whether healing places exist where wounded males can go where they will not be turned away, especially when positive change is not happening fast or fast enough. Women who have been victimized by men, women who have suffered ongoing hurt at the hands of men, naturally are wisely cautious about the energy that they can expend in the service of helping men heal. Yet there are many women who have been both helped and hurt by men. Kay Leigh Hagan testifies that the good men in her life have ruined her for man hating:

> For both men and women, Good Men can be somewhat disturbing to be around because they usually do not act in ways associated with typical men; they listen more than they talk; they self-reflect on their behavior and motives, they actively educate themselves about women's reality by seeking out women's culture and listening to women. . . . They avoid using women for vicarious emotional expression. . . . When they err—and they do err—they look to women for guidance, and receive criticism with gratitude. They practice enduring uncertainty while waiting for a new way of being to reveal previously unconsidered alternatives to controlling and abusive behavior. They intervene in other men's misogynist behavior, even when women are not present, and they work hard to recognize and challenge their own. Perhaps most amazingly, Good Men perceive the value of a feminist practice for themselves, and they advocate it not because it's polit-

> ically correct, or because they want women to like them, or even because they want women to have equality, but because they understand that male privilege prevents them not only from becoming whole, authentic human beings but also from knowing the truth about the world. . . . They offer proof that men can change.

Men like this are our true comrades in struggle. Their presence in my life sustains my hope.

Men in pain, in crisis, are calling out. If they were not calling out, we would not know that they were suffering. As we listen to their stories, we hear that they want to be well and that they do not know what to do. Based on a true story, the film *Antwone Fisher* chronicles one man's search for a path to healing. Fisher's poem "Who Will Cry for the Little Boy?" gives voice to the suffering that wounded man can no longer hide. We show our love for maleness, for men, by working to heal the wounds of men who suffer and those of us who bear witness with them. Many of us have lived the truth that recognizing the ways we are wounded is often a simpler process than finding and sustaining a practice of healing. We live in a culture where it has been accepted and even encouraged that women wholeheartedly stand by men when they are doing the work of destruction. Yet we have yet to create a world that asks us to stand by a man when he is seeking healing, when he is seeking recovery, when he is working to be a creator.

The work of male relational recovery, of reconnection, of forming intimacy and making community can never be done alone. In a world where boys and men are daily losing their way we must create guides, signposts, new paths. A culture of healing that empowers males to change is in the making. Healing does not take place in isolation. Men who love and men who long to love know this. We need to stand by them, with open hearts and open arms. We need to stand ready to hold them, offering a love that can shelter their wounded spirits as they seek to find their way home, as they exercise the will to change.